Growing Christians

*Celebrating Saints
& Holy Days at Home*

About the cover: The home altar pictured on the cover was created by the Liles family as part of their at-home celebration of the Christian year. *Photo by Allison Sandlin Liles.*

© 2020 Forward Movement
All rights reserved.
ISBN: 978-0-88028-490-5
Printed in USA

Forward Movement
inspire disciples. empower evangelists.

Growing Christians

Celebrating Saints
& Holy Days at Home

Edited by Allison Sandlin Liles

Forward Movement
Cincinnati, Ohio

Introduction

The Grow Christians community entered my life at the best possible time. I had transitioned from working full-time to part-time, taking on the role of lead parent in our household. No longer working in parish ministry, I found myself approaching our two young children as my new congregation. And I was failing. I couldn't quite find age-appropriate language to teach them about sacraments or generate excitement around celebrating feast days.

As I shared these frustrations with my son's godmother, I learned Forward Movement had an online space for parents like me—parents who wanted to nurture their children's faith formation but weren't quite sure how. In addition to teaching about our faith, early authors of GrowChristians.org paired recipes and simple crafts with liturgical feasts and lesser saints. These posts provided valuable resources to introduce holy days to my young, curious children in language they could understand. After reading encouraging posts from Derek Olsen and Nurya Love Parish, I brought my kids with me to Ash Wednesday and Good Friday services that year. I learned about books and Bibles to share with my children and godchildren and better ways to welcome and affirm other people's children while worshiping at church.

After I joined the Grow Christians community, a transition happened in our household: faith formation now primarily happened at home with Sunday school classes serving as an additional resource rather than vice versa. Every day brought new age-appropriate opportunities for worship, prayer, and formation, rather than relegating them to Sunday-only activities.

This book gathers the best of our reflections from Grow Christians on major feasts, holy days, and fasts. You can find a list of these days from the Episcopal Calendar of the Church Year found in *The Book of Common Prayer* on pages 15-33. While the church year begins on the First Sunday of Advent, the entries in this book follow the calendar year to make it easier for all households to participate and engage. Some of the feasts will be familiar to you—Easter Day, Pentecost, and Christmas Day, for example. Also included are feasts of apostles and evangelists who are lesser-known, such as Saint Matthias and Saint James of Jerusalem.

Each entry includes the appointed psalms and lessons for the day, and sometimes even with several options! On principal feast days such Christmas Day, you will see readings listed for Year A, B, and C. These letters refer to the Episcopal Church's three-year Revised Common Lectionary Cycle. On the other feast days, the readings are the same, regardless of the years, so you'll see only one set of scripture citations. We encourage you to explore the appointed readings, individually and as a household. The practice will begin to set a rhythm for engaging with scripture.

Following the readings are reflections by a diverse group of authors: moms and dads, godparents and grandparents, friends and youth group leaders, all bound by their commitment to helping form young people in the faith. These writers come from across the church and are both ordained and lay, from households that take a variety of shapes. The reflections share authentic stories of successes and failures, of the struggle and triumph in loving children and modeling for them the love of God.

Each day also includes a response activity to do with children. Many of these activities will appeal to young children as well as teenagers. However, I invite you to adapt the reflections and responses to fit your needs. The day offers a section to learn more, to dive deeper into the history and context of the day. We have created a page on our website with additional resources to support your activities. Visit GrowChristians.org/holydays to learn more.

And finally, each day concludes with a prayer. Most of these prayers are from the latest iteration of Lesser Feasts and Fasts, but as noted, some are from *The Book of Common Prayer*. Prayer is a central component of our lives of faith and a wonderful habit to cultivate within your household.

Welcome to our Grow Christians community. Please join us online by following Grow Christians on Facebook or subscribing to receive posts by email at GrowChristians.org. My hope is that this community and the resources and wisdom it offers will be as transformational for you and your household as it has been for mine.

Allison Sandlin Liles, Editor

Calendar of Holy Days
and Major Feasts and Fasts

January
1   The Holy Name of Our Lord Jesus Christ
6   The Epiphany of Our Lord Jesus Christ
18   The Confession of Saint Peter the Apostle
25   The Conversion of Saint Paul the Apostle

February
2   The Presentation of
        Our Lord Jesus Christ in the Temple
    Ash Wednesday *
24   Saint Matthias the Apostle

March
19   Saint Joseph
25   The Annunciation of Our Lord Jesus Christ
        to the Blessed Virgin Mary

April
    Palm Sunday *
    Maundy Thursday *
    Good Friday *
    Holy Saturday *
    Easter Day *
25   Saint Mark the Evangelist

May

1   Saint Philip and Saint James, Apostles
     Ascension Day *
     Day of Pentecost *
31   The Visitation of the Blessed Virgin Mary

June

     Trinity Sunday *
11   Saint Barnabas the Apostle
24   The Nativity of Saint John the Baptist
29   Saint Peter and Saint Paul, Apostles

July

4   Independence Day (USA)
22   Saint Mary Magdalene
25   Saint James the Apostle

August

6   The Transfiguration of Our Lord Jesus Christ
15   Saint Mary the Virgin,
          Mother of Our Lord Jesus Christ
24   Saint Bartholomew the Apostle

September

14   Holy Cross Day
21   Saint Matthew, Apostle and Evangelist
29   Saint Michael and All Angels

Growing Christians

October

18   Saint Luke the Evangelist
23   Saint James of Jerusalem,
                Brother of Our Lord Jesus Christ, and Martyr
28   Saint Simon and Saint Jude, Apostles

November

 1   All Saints
        Thanksgiving Day (USA) *
30   Saint Andrew the Apostle

December

21   Saint Thomas the Apostle
25   The Nativity of Our Lord Jesus Christ
26   Saint Stephen, Deacon and Martyr
27   Saint John, Apostle and Evangelist
28   The Holy Innocents

These dates change each year. Check your calendar to determine the date.

The Holy Name of Our Lord Jesus Christ

Read

Psalm 8 | Numbers 6:22-27 | Galatians 4:4-7 *or*
Philippians 2:5-11 | Luke 2:15-21

Reflect

Today, eight days into the Christmas season, the Episcopal Church celebrates the Feast of the Holy Name. We celebrate this feast day on January 1 each year because it's the day when Jesus was named by his parents and circumcised. In the gospel appointed for today, we learn "eight days (after his birth) had passed, it was time to circumcise the child; and he was called Jesus, the name given by the angel before he was conceived in the womb." This sentence informs us that Mary and Joseph were devout Jews, as it was the Law of Moses requiring all newborn boys to be circumcised when they were eight days old (Leviticus 12:3).

> ### Author
>
> **Allison Sandlin Liles** is a wife, mother, peacemaker, and priest learning how to navigate life in the suburban wilds of Dallas.

For centuries this feast day was called the Feast of the Circumcision. Our 1979 *Book of Common Prayer* adjusted the name, emphasizing the naming of Jesus over the circumcising of Jesus. It was customary at the time of circumcision for family and friends to witness parents publicly name the child. This is a tradition that we as modern-day Episcopalians have retained. Our liturgy of baptism begins with parents and godparents presenting the person to be baptized by naming them aloud.

Jesus is a name our children know well. It's the name toddlers confidently shout whenever they are asked a question during children's chapel. It's the baby's name lying in the manger who children crowd around to glimpse during nativity pageants. It's a name our children already know, but today we have the opportunity to teach them more about it.

Jesus is a Greek transliteration of the Hebrew name Joshua, or *Yehoshuah*. When the angel Gabriel tells Joseph to name the child in Mary's womb *Yeshua*, Joseph would have known it meant "God saves" or "deliverer." It's a heavy name for a young child to carry around, and I wonder how Jesus felt about it.

But Jesus isn't the only name for God's son in the Bible. We're offered so many more throughout the Old and New Testaments.

The Vine
The Messiah
The Good Shepherd
Living Water
The Word

The Bread of Life

Prince of Peace

With all the names we have for God's Son, Jesus remains the most important. Jesus is the salvation of the world, just as his name implies. When we celebrate the Holy Name of Jesus, we are celebrating the one through whom and in whom the Lord helps and saves his people. And as Jesus' disciples, we minister in his holy name to the world around us.

Respond

Spend some time today talking through the many holy names for Jesus with the children in your life. My children engage conversations more fully if their hands are busy, so we made ornaments with the names of Jesus. My church created these ornaments by coloring a printable template (thecraftyclassroom.com), then slathering them with Mod Podge during an intergenerational Advent party. The children immediately recognized some of the names for Jesus, but others were unfamiliar to them like Rose of Sharon and Shiloh. If those names are new to you as well, never fear! With the help of Oremus Bible Browser's search feature (bible.oremus.org), you can enter each specific name and find where it appears in the Bible.

Learn More

The designation of this day as the Feast of the Holy Name was new to the 1979 revision of *The Book of Common Prayer*. Previous Anglican Prayer Books called it the Feast of the Circumcision. January 1 is, of course, the eighth day after Christmas Day, and the Gospel according to Luke records that eight days after his birth the child was circumcised and given the name Jesus.

The liturgical commemoration of the Circumcision is of Gallican origin, and a Council of Tours in 567 enacted that the day was to be kept as a fast day to counteract pagan festivities connected with the beginning of the new year. In the Roman tradition, January 1 was observed as the octave day of Christmas, and it was particularly devoted to the Virgin Mary.

The early preachers of the gospel lay stress on the name as showing that Jesus was a man of flesh and blood, though also the Son of God, who died a human death, and whom God raised from death (Acts 2:32; 4:12). The name "Jesus" was given to him, as the angel explained to Joseph, because he would "save his people from their sins" (Matthew 1:21) as the name means "Savior" or "Deliverer" in Hebrew.

Then, as now, people longed to be freed from evils: political, social, and spiritual. The name of Jesus calls to mind the true freedom that is ours through Jesus Christ.

Pray

Eternal Father, you gave to your incarnate Son the holy name of Jesus to be the sign of our salvation: Plant in every heart, we pray, the love of him who is the Savior of the world, our Lord Jesus Christ; who lives and reigns with you and the Holy Spirit, one God, in glory everlasting. *Amen.*

The Epiphany of Our Lord Jesus Christ

Read

Psalm 72:1-7, 10-14 | Isaiah 60:1-9
Ephesians 3:1-12 | Matthew 2:1-12

Reflect

Arise, shine; for your light has come,
*   and the glory of the Lord has risen upon you.*
For darkness shall cover the earth,
*   and thick darkness the peoples;*
but the Lord will arise upon you,
*   and his glory will appear over you.*

Author

Miriam Willard McKenney finds extreme joy in parenting her three girls: Nia, Kaia, and Jaiya. She and her husband, David, met at the Union of Black Episcopalians conference in 1981.

Confession: celebrating Epiphany wasn't part of my family's culture until recently. Growing up, we waited until January 6 to move the three kings to the manger, and we were never in a rush to take down our decorations. But we didn't talk about the meaning behind these traditions.

One new thing I started last year was reading the lectionary for Epiphany and talking about Isaiah 60:1-6 with my girls. I love talking with kids about the myriad connections throughout the Old and New Testaments. It's like a giant dot-to-dot that they slowly connect, sometimes missing a few dots that they come back to later. The more dots they connect brings the picture of a life with Christ into focus.

Nations shall come to your light,
and kings to the brightness of your dawn.

There's something magical that happens when my girls or youth group kids read scripture containing fulfilled prophecy. Their eyes widen, there's often a gasp—God's word reveals itself to them and they receive the revelation. There are lots of opportunity for that with Isaiah 60:1-6. We like to imagine that God is speaking to baby Jesus.

Lift up your eyes and look around;
they all gather together, they come to you;
your sons shall come from far away,
and your daughters shall be carried on their nurses' arms.

Just as our parenting begins on the day we receive the gifts known as our children, God's parenting of Jesus begins. God says to Jesus, "Wake up, little baby, and look around… see who has come to visit you!" Do you remember saying something like that to your babies and toddlers when family and friends came to see your miracle of new life? Then God reminds Jesus that he is special and will have generations after him who will love, honor, and bless him.

Then you shall see and be radiant;
your heart shall thrill and rejoice,

because the abundance of the sea shall be brought to you,
the wealth of the nations shall come to you.

We want our children to know they're special. They're full of endless possibilities, hopes, dreams, and promises. As parents, we want them to have everything they'll need to be successful. God is no different. Jesus' father wants him to know that the world would be his, before he became the world's. I believe this is at the heart of what we celebrate on Epiphany. God shows his son to the world—the secret's out. The mystery is revealed.

A multitude of camels shall cover you,
the young camels of Midian and Ephah;
all those from Sheba shall come.
They shall bring gold and frankincense,
and shall proclaim the praise of the Lord.

Think back to when you brought your baby home. What was your main concern? I wanted my children to be safe and protected. One way that God protects our children is through the members of our village—that special group consisting of our family, close friends, and faith community. Jesus' village included the three kings, who teach us how to celebrate, honor, and protect our children.

Epiphany offers us a chance to remember that Jesus was a king but not the king people thought he would be. He was a baby, a child of God, and his life promised that we, too, would all be children of God. The prophets foretold him, God revealed him, the three kings honored him, and we adore him.

Respond

Some faith communities bless chalk on Epiphany and hand it out to the congregation for people to write a blessing on their homes. Traditionally, the chalking is done above the door and takes this form: 20+C+M+B+21, in which "21" is replaced by the current year. The letters are the abbreviation for the Latin phrase *Christus mansionem benedicat*—Christ bless this house. (A second meaning and mnemonic device is "Caspar, Melchior, and Balthazar," the traditional names for the Magi). The + signs represent the cross, and 20-21 is the year. If you want to take the activity one step further, you can find instructions on how to make your chalk (diynetwork.com).

The following prayer is traditionally used for the blessing of chalk:

Loving God, bless this chalk which you have created, that it may be helpful to your people; and grant through the invocation of your most Holy Name that we who use it in faith to write upon the door of our home the names of your holy ones Caspar, Melchior, and Balthazar, may receive health of body and protection of soul for all who dwell in or visit our home; through Jesus Christ our Lord. Amen.

Learn More

The name "Epiphany" is derived from a Greek word meaning manifestation or appearing. Anglican prayer books interpret the word as "The Manifestation of Christ to the Gentiles." The

Growing Christians

last phrase, of course, is a reference to the story of the Magi from the East.

A Christian observance on January 6 is found as early as the end of the second century in Egypt. The feast combined commemorations of three events that were considered manifestations of the Incarnate Lord: the visit of the Magi, led by the star of Bethlehem; the baptism of Jesus in the waters of the Jordan River; and Jesus' first recorded miracle, the changing of water into wine at the wedding of Cana.

Epiphany is still the primary Feast of the Incarnation in Eastern churches, and the three-fold emphasis is still prominent. In the West, however, including Anglican churches, the story of the Magi has tended to overshadow the other two events. Modern lectionary reform, reflected in the 1979 Prayer Book, has recovered the primitive trilogy by setting the event of Christ's Baptism as the theme of the First Sunday after the Epiphany in all three years, and by providing the story of the Miracle at Cana as the gospel for the second Sunday after the Epiphany in Year C.

Pray

O God, by the leading of a star you manifested your only Son to the peoples of the earth: Lead us, who know you now by faith, to your presence, where we may see your glory face to face; through Jesus Christ our Lord, who lives and reigns with you and the Holy Spirit, one God, now and for ever. *Amen.*

The Confession of Saint Peter the Apostle

Read

Psalm 23 | Acts 4:8-13 | 1 Peter 5:1-4 | Matthew 16:13-19

Reflect

In Shakespeare's famous tragedy, "Romeo and Juliet," Juliet asks a question that endures through the ages. Swimming in a sea of emotions and hormones and realizing that the man she loves is a member of a rival family, love-struck Juliet asks, "What's in a name? A rose by any other name would smell as sweet."

> ### Author
>
> **Marcus Halley** is an Episcopal priest serving as dean of formation for the Diocese of Connecticut.

The subtext here is that names are meaningless. Surely getting involved in a hasty relationship is worth more than potential family turmoil and premature death, right?

The gospels might bear a counter-witness. When Jesus asks his disciples in Matthew 16, "Who do you say that I am?", Simon Peter is the only one to respond with the correct answer: "You are the Messiah, the Son of the living God."

This moment of divine clarity is where Simon Peter, one of the first disciples called to follow Jesus, becomes an icon of the fledgling movement of Jesus. It is a statement of faith more than a statement of fact, and that faith is the rock upon which Jesus builds his church.

What I appreciate the most about Simon Peter is not his rockiness but his softness, his porousness, and his jaggedness. He is brash. He is impatient. He is rude. He is so incredibly human. One of my favorite stories involving Simon Peter has nothing to do with the time he had great faith but the time he could've used a great deal more.

Just two chapters earlier, in Matthew 14, the evangelist captures the story of Peter stepping out into the stormy sea. He is so sure of himself. He walks forward on the white-crested waves until he takes his eyes off Jesus and begins to look at the mess he has gotten himself into. As he sinks, Jesus reaches forth his hand to save him. "You of little faith," Jesus says. "Why did you doubt?"

Jesus builds his church on the confession of a man with a sketchy record of firm faith. In this moment, Peter is so sure that Jesus is the Christ, the son of the living God, but in just a few chapters, he will deny he even knows Jesus. This solid rock appears to show a few cracks.

But Jesus builds the church on that rock anyway. It might be true that the rhythm of faith and doubt are simply two sides of the same coin of relationship with Jesus. There are times where we experience something of the divine that makes our faith seem firm. Other times, it tends to feel less secure. Either way, when we fail to believe in ourselves, it is comforting to know that Jesus still believes in us. As a popular maxim suggests, those cracks in our faith might be how the light of Christ gets in to invite us into deeper awareness and more glorious revelation.

The Confession of Saint Peter is a snapshot in the life of an apostle who would have many more ups and downs before finally being crucified upside down in Rome. It reveals a truth: in the eyes of Christ, we are never identified by the worst thing we have ever done; rather, Jesus knows us as the best we can possibly be.

Respond

Peter's time with Jesus was rocky—to say the least! But Jesus says that Peter is the rock upon which the church will be built. And ultimately, he becomes just that, spreading the gospel near and far with his travels. Spend some time with rocks today. You might collect some on a walk and place them in a flower bed as a reminder or decorate and place them in your neighborhood for someone else to find (rhythmsofplay.com). You could make some rocks with playdough or modeling clay. Or you might get really creative and bake edible fudge rocks— or rock-shaped cookies or biscuits (edible fudge rock recipe: hungryhappenings.com)

Learn More

When Jesus' disciple Simon confessed, "You are the Christ," Jesus responded, "You are Peter, and on this rock I will build my church." This fisherman and his brother Andrew were the first disciples called by Jesus. Peter figures prominently in the gospels, often stumbling, impetuous, intense, and uncouth.

It was Peter who attempted to walk on the sea and began to sink; it was Peter who impulsively wished to build three tabernacles on the mountain of the Transfiguration; it was Peter who, just before the crucifixion, three times denied knowing his Lord.

But it was also Peter who, after Pentecost, risked his life to do the Lord's work, speaking boldly of his belief in Jesus. It was also Peter, the Rock, whose strength and courage helped the young church in its questioning about the mission beyond the Jewish community. Opposed at first to the baptism of Gentiles, he had the humility to admit a change of heart and to baptize the Roman centurion Cornelius and his household. Even after this, Peter had a continuing struggle with his conservatism, for Paul, writing to the Galatians, rebukes him for giving way to the demands of Jewish Christians to dissociate himself from table-fellowship with Gentiles.

Though the New Testament makes no mention of it, the tradition connecting Peter with Rome is early and credible. According to a legend based on that tradition, Peter fled from Rome during the persecution under Nero. On the Appian Way, he met Christ, and asked him, "*Domine, quo vadis?*"

("Lord, where are you going?"). Jesus answered, "I am coming to be crucified again." Peter thereupon retraced his steps, and was shortly thereafter crucified, head downwards. "I am not worthy to be crucified as my Lord was," he is supposed to have said.

As we watch Peter struggle with himself, often stumble, love his Lord and deny him, speak rashly and act impetuously, his life reminds us that our Lord did not come to save the godly and strong but to save the weak and the sinful. Simon, an ordinary human being, was transformed by the Holy Spirit into the "Rock," and became the leader of the Church.

Since 1908, the eight days between the feast of the Confession of Saint Peter and the feast of the Conversion of Saint Paul have been observed ecumenically as the Week of Prayer for Christian Unity.

Pray

Almighty Father, who inspired Simon Peter, first among the apostles, to confess Jesus as Messiah and Son of the living God: Keep your Church steadfast upon the rock of this faith, so that in unity and peace we may proclaim the one truth and follow the one Lord, our Savior Jesus Christ; who lives and reigns with you and the Holy Spirit, one God, now and for ever. *Amen.*

The Conversion of Saint Paul the Apostle

Read

Psalm 27 | Acts 26:9-21
Galatians 1:11-24 | Matthew 10:16-22

Reflect

Why Saul? Of all the people of the early church who are working to spread the news of Christ's life, ministry, death, and resurrection...why does Jesus choose Saul to become one of the most remembered and quoted saints?

Most of us know the story, told three times in the book of Acts (chapters 9, 22, and 26). But I think we need to backtrack to the stoning of Stephen in Acts 7 and one oft-forgotten but profound sentence at the very beginning of Acts 8 to understand the significance of the conversion of Saint Paul, celebrated January 25.

> **Author**
>
> **Christina (Tina) Clark** lives in Denver, Colorado, has two teenage sons, and loves all things church, the Rocky Mountains, and the Pacific Ocean.

Saul is a tentmaker (Acts 18:3) from Tarsus, born into a Jewish family and raised in the strict Jewish sect known as the Pharisees, who were devoted to an unbending adherence to

Mosaic law. We first hear of Saul at the end of Acts 7, when he observes Stephen being stoned to death. He is not described as a participant, but he is brought to our attention as more than a disinterested bystander:

Then they dragged him out of the city and began to stone him; and the witnesses laid their coats at the feet of a young man named Saul. (Acts 7:58)

And Saul approved of their killing him. (Acts 8:1)

Thus begins Saul's targeted and energetic persecutions of all who proclaim the word. Saul is described as "ravaging the church by entering house after house, dragging off both men and women, [and] committing them to prison."

Saul seems to be in the grips of a manic lust for the downfall of Christ's followers. Like the apostles before him, who drop their fishing nets to follow Jesus, Saul abandons his life as a tentmaker to chase, track down, and imprison Christ's followers, even asking for letters from the high priest so that he can go to Damascus to continue his campaign against the disciples of the Lord.

And that's where it happens. On the road to Damascus, Jesus stops Saul in his tracks by appearing as a blinding light, brighter than the midday sun, and striking Saul blind. And Jesus asks, "Saul, Saul, why do you persecute me?" (Acts 9:1-4)

This is a Bible story I think we neglect to share with children. What kid doesn't like a story in which the evil villain is struck down supernaturally? And kids relate deeply to stories of redemption because they need to know our love is constant no matter how big their mistakes. But I think the real question, the most critical part of the story, is the least considered:

Why Saul?

Shouldn't Saul be vanquished? In the underdeveloped plots of most kids' movies, Saul would fall to an inevitable but unseen death at the bottom of a deep chasm or be swept away, again nonviolently, in a stormy sea. But that's not how God works through the Son and Savior Jesus Christ. Christ came to save us, not to vanquish us. When we are figuratively blind to the word of God, Christ continues to love us and to work toward removing the scales from our eyes.

Why Saul?

Because we are all, in our own times and in different ways, Saul.

And in Saul I often recognize the passionate energy of my boys and so many other children I've worked with over the years. Fiery children who seek almost constant sensory input and are incessantly busy. These are children who are never going to sit quietly at their desk and write organized thoughts in their journals but whose imaginations brim endlessly with stories too big to fit in the confines of a pencil and a spiral notebook.

Like Saul, these are the children with the strongest potential to change the world. Given a solid foundation of compassion, empathy, love of God and neighbor, these children will be the problem-solvers and peacemakers of the next generation. After all, after his encounter with Christ, Saul becomes Saint Paul, one of the most prolific, vigorous, and passionate proclaimers of Christ's message.

So we must embrace and guide the fervent, if exhausting, energy of our passionate children. We must fuel them with the stories of our faith and teach them to see and speak against injustice. We can help these kids build strong hearts for empathy and compassion by engaging them in outreach, using their energetic creativity to raise up those Jesus called "the least of my brothers and sisters." These young Sauls, brought up in the Word of Christ and taught to know and embrace the inspiration of the Holy Spirit, have the potential to match Saint Paul in energy and courage. Thanks be to God.

Respond

The Confession of Saint Peter and the Conversion of Saint Paul provide the bookends for the Week of Prayer for Christian Unity. Whether you observe this week of intentional prayer every January or you are learning about it for the first time right now, offer a prayer today for the unifying mission of all followers of Jesus Christ.

Holy God, source of all life, help us acknowledge and embrace our diversity and our oneness. We pray that as your followers we might celebrate our differences as we seek to serve you on common ground. Just as you experienced through the incarnation of Jesus

Christ, our world can be a hurtful place. As this Week of Prayer for Christian Unity draws to a close, we pray that you fill our hearts with courage, love, and humility as we work together for justice and peace. May your hope in a more just future unite all our thoughts and decisions, and bring peace. Amen.

Learn More

Paul, or Saul as he was known until he became a Christian, was a Roman citizen, born in Tarsus, in present-day Turkey. He was brought up as an observant Jew, studying in Jerusalem for a time under Gamaliel, the most famous rabbi of the day. Describing himself, he said, "I am an Israelite, a descendant of Abraham, a member of the tribe of Benjamin" (Romans 11:1).

A few years after the death of Jesus, Saul came in contact with the new Christian movement, and became one of the most fanatical of those who were determined to stamp out this "dangerous heresy." Saul witnessed the stoning of Stephen and approved of it. He was on the way to Damascus to lead in further persecution of the Christians when his dramatic conversion took place.

From that day, Paul devoted his life totally to Christ, and especially to the conversion of Gentiles. The Acts of the Apostles describes the courage and determination with which he planted Christian congregations over a large area of the land bordering the eastern Mediterranean.

His letters, which are the earliest Christian writings, established him as one of the early founders of Christian theology. He writes, "I have been crucified with Christ; it is no longer I who live, but Christ who lives in me; and the life I now live in the flesh I live by faith in the Son of God, who loved me and gave himself for me" (Galatians 2:19b-20).

Paul describes himself as small and insignificant in appearance: "His letters are weighty and strong," it was said of him, "but his bodily presence is weak, and his speech of no account" (2 Corinthians 10:10). He writes of having a disability or affliction which he had prayed God to remove from him, and quotes the Lord's reply, "My grace is sufficient for you, for my power is made perfect in weakness."

Therefore, Paul went on to say, "I will boast all the more gladly of my weaknesses, so that the power of Christ may dwell in me" (2 Corinthians 12:9b).

Paul is believed to have been martyred at Rome in the year 64 under Nero.

The feast of the Conversion of Saint Paul marks the end of the Week of Prayer for Christian Unity.

Pray

O God, who by the preaching of your apostle Paul has caused the light of the Gospel to shine throughout the world: Grant, we pray, that we, having his wonderful conversion in remembrance, may show ourselves thankful to you by following his holy teaching; through Jesus Christ our Lord, who lives and reigns with you, in the unity of the Holy Spirit, one God, now and for ever. *Amen.*

The Presentation of Our Lord Jesus Christ in the Temple

Read

Psalm 84 *or* 24:7-10 | Malachi 3:1-4
Hebrews 2:14-18 | Luke 2:22-40

Reflect

At some point in his life, Simeon receives a promise from the Holy Spirit that he will not die until he sees the Messiah. Luke's Gospel tells us that the Holy Spirit rests on him and guides him into Jerusalem's temple on the very day Mary and Joseph arrive to present Jesus to the Lord. Then it happens. Simeon sees Jesus. The sight of the child, the mere arrival of the promised one, moves the old, devout, righteous man to song. Simeon takes Jesus in his arms and praises God, knowing that glory will indeed be brought to his people, providing "a light of revelation to the Gentiles."

I came to know the Song of Simeon through praying Compline as an eight-year-old at the Diocese of Alabama's Camp McDowell. The

Author

Allison Sandlin Liles is a wife, mother, peacemaker, and priest learning how to navigate life in the suburban wilds of Dallas, Texas.

Song of Simeon is the canticle option in the nighttime Daily Office service found in our *Book of Common Prayer* and is prayed every summer night at Camp McDowell. The English translation of its Latin name, *Nunc dimittis,* forms the first words of the song "now let depart."

Every night of my first camp session, just as homesickness started to seep in, I found comfort and peace sitting on hard wooden pews in an old stone chapel with fans rotating the stifling August air. The waters of Clear Creek rolled over the dam below the chapel while a counselor led us through the ancient night prayers of Compline. After a few more summers at camp, these prayers and songs were written on my heart.

The simple act of chanting a canticle as a child became a spiritual tool for the rest of my life. As someone often told by childhood teachers, "Oh honey, why don't you just mouth the words rather than sing them," I cherish my college summers working at Camp McDowell when I learned to harmonize the Song of Simeon in the stone chapel.

I carried this song with me to Virginia Seminary where I was completely shocked to learn that our camp setting wasn't found in any current hymnals of the Episcopal Church, so I taught it to my classmates. As a new priest back in Alabama, I sang the *Nunc dimittis* with dying church members, who like Simeon, contentedly sought eternal peace. As a new mom, I sang Simeon's words to my children as we rocked during nighttime feedings, and now we sing them together after bedtime reading and back scratches. I sang them with my godson when he was just two years old because his mother's priesthood was also profoundly shaped by Camp McDowell, and she had already taught him.

This simple song is written on my heart and carried with me everywhere.

Simeon doesn't see any flashy miracles in the temple that day. Water isn't turned into wine. A dead man bound in cloth doesn't rise from the grave. Simeon simply sees baby Jesus, God incarnate, and sings, "Lord, now let your servant depart in peace according to your Word, for my eyes have seen your salvation which has been prepared for all people." He sees the Christ child with his own eyes and finds fulfillment.

Most of parenthood is like this for me. The earth-shaking miracles and wonders are few and far between, but the glimpses of God happen right before my eyes every single day.

When I see my daughter picking up litter without any fanfare or prompting, I see Eve tending the garden. When my son offers his school snack to the person seeking food outside our car window, I see Jesus feeding one of the five thousand. When my husband sits on our bed playing his guitar while our daughter dances wildly around him, I see Miriam and Moses singing out their praises after the waters swallow Pharaoh's army. When our family attended Camp McDowell in August and sang the Song of Simeon in the stone chapel with two hundred fellow children of God, I felt like faithful Simeon seeing God with his own eyes.

Our families show us God in everyday life, but I worry we are too busy looking for flashy miracles and mountaintop experiences to notice. Recognizing and naming these everyday moments is critical for our faith and the faith of our children. Equally important is remembering that we are showing God to our families through our seemingly simple actions. It could be a song that you teach them tonight, the conversation driving home from an Ash Wednesday service in two weeks, or the prayer note you tuck into lunchboxes each morning before school.

One seemingly simple act in childhood has the potential to become a spiritual tool for the rest of their lives.

Respond

What prayers do you carry with you? Is it a song or a prayer for a specific person? Using large pieces of paper, cut out hearts for each member of your household, and inscribe the prayers written on your hearts. Search YouTube for a video of the Song of Simeon. Learn the words and sing along!

Learn More

Today's feast is sometimes known as the Purification of Saint Mary the Virgin and also as Candlemas. In the Orthodox Church, it has also been called the Meeting of Christ with Simeon. Such a variety of names is ample testimony to the wealth of spiritual meaning that generations of Christians have discovered in this small incident.

The title "The Presentation" reminds us of the Jewish law (Exodus 13:2; 22:29) that every firstborn son had to be dedicated to God in memory of the Israelites' deliverance from Egypt, when the firstborn sons of the Egyptians died and those of Israel were spared.

When Mary placed her infant son into the arms of Simeon, it was the meeting of the Old and New Dispensations. The old sacrifices, the burnt offerings and oblations, were done away with; a new and perfect offering had come into the temple. God had provided himself a lamb for the burnt offering (Genesis 22:8), his only Son. The offering was to be made once for all on the cross. At every Eucharist those who are in Christ recall that sinless offering and unite "themselves, their souls and bodies" with the self-oblation of their Lord and Savior.

It is traditional that candles are blessed on this day, for use throughout the rest of the year, which is why the feast is also sometimes known as "Candlemas."

Pray

Almighty and everliving God, we humbly pray that, as your only-begotten Son was this day presented in the temple, so we may be presented to you with pure and clean hearts by Jesus Christ our Lord; who lives and reigns with you and the Holy Spirit, one God, now and for ever. *Amen.*

*This date changes each year.
Check your calendar to
determine the date.*

Read

Psalm 103 *or* 103:8-14 | Joel 2:1-2, 12-17 *or* Isaiah 58:1-12
2 Corinthians 5:20b—6:10 | Matthew 6:1-6, 16-21

Reflect

As a child, I was somewhat confused about death. I blame *Star Wars.*

The original *Star Wars* movie came out when I was three; seeing it with my family remains one of my earliest memories. My meditation on the movie continued over a comic-book adaptation of the story that I read over and over until it finally fell apart from over-reading a couple of years later. My first conscious experience of "death" was Obi Wan Kenobi cut down by Darth Vader in a dramatic lightsaber duel—and his subsequent disappearance.

Author

Derek Olsen holds a doctorate in New Testament and lives in Baltimore, Maryland, with his wife, an Episcopal priest, and their two daughters.

Thus, I thought that's what everybody did when they died: their body just vanished like Ben Kenobi's.

Around that time, my maternal grandfather passed away. I was so puzzled when my mom and dad told me that they were going to the viewing; I distinctly remember wondering, "Since he disappeared, what is it that they are going to go see…?"

Parents might be reluctant to take their children to a service like Ash Wednesday because of its thematic content; the two big things on tap are death and sin. If they're anything like me at that age, your kids have already been exposed to the concept of death, if only in movies. Indeed, if your kids have seen the virtually obligatory Disney canon, they've seen death used as a plot device that turns on them understanding something about it. Think of the shooting of Bambi's mom or the crushing of Ray the Cajun firefly in *The Princess and the Frog*.

Since my wife is an Episcopal priest, I'm the parent responsible for taking our two girls to church, managing them in the pew by myself, keeping them attentive (or at least relatively quiet), and answering any questions that might come up. I know what it's like to get the questions; I've handled the questions (including an age-appropriate explanation of the whole "Bathsheba" incident). And, yes, even as a theologically trained biblical scholar, I find myself fumbling for words or saying, "uh—I'll get back to you on that…" But what I have learned is that the kids already have questions about these things; what they hear in the service provides them an opportunity to ask about a topic they've encountered but don't understand. Death is one of those.

I never asked my parents about death or the whole "disappearing" thing. But I wish I had—or that they would have discussed it with me. I had to figure it out. I've tried to have these discussions so my girls won't be in the same boat I was. Now, there's something to be said for sheltering your kids from graphic depictions of death and violence. However, these unpleasant realities are facts of the world we live in. There's a difference between sheltering kids from content versus sheltering them from concepts. They don't need to see the pictures, but they do need to understand what happens in the world around them.

With the topics we don't feel comfortable talking to our kids about—let's just call out death and sex as two of the biggies— we can cling to the illusion that if we don't bring them up, our kids will never know about them. But the combination of pop culture and conversation with friends makes this a losing strategy in the long term. If you don't do the educating, the entertainment industry will. My preference has always been to have brief, periodic, age-appropriate conversations about big topics like these. Clear and honest conversation on difficult topics is way better than glossing over them in silence and praying for ignorance.

Thus, Ash Wednesday services and the resulting questions provide an opportunity for honest communication with your kids to clear up misunderstandings about life and death—or sin—they may have absorbed from movies, TV, or friends.

However, another major piece of parental discomfort with Ash Wednesday is all about sheltering but isn't focused on the kids. It's about us. We're trying to shelter ourselves.

Ash Wednesday is a difficult but necessary part of the Christian proclamation. It wrestles with stuff that we work very hard to avoid. Nobody likes to think about death or sin, but Ash Wednesday puts these things front and center. If there's anything that I want to avoid more than my own mortality, it's my kids' mortality.

My younger daughter was born at the end of February. Her very first trip outside our house was going to the church my wife served for Ash Wednesday. Let me tell you: it's a cold hard slap of reality to see a cross of ash on the forehead of your newborn. Some members of the congregation were shocked that we even brought her up and questioned if such a thing was even appropriate. But it is. Death is a part of life. Mortality is a part of reality.

Bringing your kids to Ash Wednesday services means that you will receive the reminder that your kids will die. Some day. Hopefully, a very long time from now. I, for one, don't like to be reminded that my girls will die. But Ash Wednesday confronts me with that fact. The great Anglican spiritual teacher Evelyn Underhill once defined mysticism as the art of bringing the self into union with reality. The mystic—the truly spiritual person—is one who embraces that challenge. And that means facing reality, not fleeing it, and all of its hard edges.

Growing Christians

The gospel calls us to open up our lives, to live honestly in light of what the world is and who God is. The truth of the gospel means wrestling with truths that we don't like. There's a natural inclination to hide them from our kids—and from ourselves. But, through the rhythm of the liturgical year, including Ash Wednesday, the church calls us to an integrity about ourselves, about the world around us, and about God.

Only if we're willing to tell the whole truth about sin and death are we able to tell the whole truth about resurrection.

Bring your kids to Ash Wednesday. Let them see and hear and participate in the church's admission of the hard edges of reality: that we sin; that we die. Let them ask you questions about what all of that means. Answer honestly—even if it's a solemn, heartfelt "I've got no clue…"

Hear the invitation to keep a holy Lent as an invitation to study the hard edges of life with the conviction that a robust faith helps us grapple with reality as it is, not flee it for more comfortable and comforting fantasies.

Come to hear the truth—for the truth will set you free.

Respond

This year try the daily spiritual practice of coloring a prayer calendar during Lent. Sybil Macbeth, author of *Praying in Color*, offers Lenten calendar templates that allow you to focus on one word or person each day. There is an empty box for each day of Lent where you may write the word or name, then color around it while praying. You might use a word from daily scripture readings or create a gratitude list. This is a prayer practice, not a journey toward creating a beautiful work of art. For children (and many adults!), busy eyes and hands allow the mind to better focus on prayer. Search for Sybil MacBeth's printable Lenten calendar templates online.

Learn more

Ash Wednesday marks the beginning of the forty days of Lent. If you attend a worship service today, you'll hear clergy invite those gathered into an observance of a holy Lent. This invitation is an ancient one, as Christians have devoted themselves to preparing for the celebration of Easter since the days of the early Church. Through prayer, fasting, and self-reflection, we are invited to spend Lent recognizing and confessing our mortality, our sinfulness, and God's gift of everlasting life. Following this invitation, we come forward to receive the imposition of ashes marked in the shape of a cross on our foreheads. These ashes signify repentance and mourning as read about in the biblical books of Job, Joel, and Esther. We carry on this tradition of wearing ashes to reflect our commitment to living as members of the Jesus Movement as we embark on this solemn season of Lent.

Pray

Almighty and everlasting God, you hate nothing you have made and forgive the sins of all who are penitent: Create and make in us new and contrite hearts, that we, worthily lamenting our sins and acknowledging our wretchedness, may obtain of you, the God of all mercy, perfect remission and forgiveness; through Jesus Christ our Lord, who lives and reigns with you and the Holy Spirit, one God, for ever and ever. *Amen.*

—*The Book of Common Prayer*

Saint Matthias the Apostle

Read

Psalm 15 | Acts 1:15-26
Philippians 3:13b-21 | John 15:1, 6-16

Reflect

"Therefore, we must select one of those who have accompanied us during the whole time the Lord Jesus lived among us..."
—Acts 1:21 CEB

Author

Dorian Del Priore is an Episcopal priest who has been involved in youth ministry for more than twenty years. Dorian is a husband to Lauren and a father to Jordan and Brynn, and they live in Columbia, South Carolina.

Very little is known about Saint Matthias, as he is only mentioned in the first chapter of Acts when he is selected (by casting lots) to replace Judas as an apostle. Early church fathers believe that he was among the seventy-two sent out by Jesus, but the only thing we know for sure about Matthias is this: he followed Jesus from the beginning and was present throughout the ministry of Jesus.

There are little nuggets like this throughout the New Testament that are easy to overlook. We know the disciples answered the call of Jesus and followed him, but it is easy to forget or recognize there were others, too. In the midst of the crowds that gathered in villages and followed Jesus around, there were those who followed him from the beginning, accompanying Jesus and the disciples along their journey. I wonder…how big was this following?

That there was this other group following Jesus and the disciples is fascinating to me. They would have witnessed so very much: each and every teaching, each and every miracle, the events in Jerusalem, the tomb, the resurrection, and the ascension. They were faithful from the beginning.

Matthias and Justus must have been upstanding individuals to be considered for the mantle of apostle. However, at the most basic level, they were present, and they were faithful. Simply put, they were willing to show up.

When I was a relatively new full-time youth minister, I attended a meeting with other youth ministers at our diocesan office. During these gatherings over lunch, we vented our frustrations, shared ideas, and developed community. At some point during one of the meetings, a senior priest on staff at the cathedral poked his head into the room. He was asked to share a word of wisdom with us.

"More than 90 percent of youth ministry is just showing up."

It was both very simple and quite profound. I'm sure more was said, however, his core point stuck: showing up, faithfully and reliably, is vitally important. This is true for all types of ministry.

And this is the ministry of Matthias. He followed faithfully. He showed up reliably. He was present consistently. This is what the mission of the church and the call of Jesus requires: showing up. When we show up, with an open heart and open hands, we cultivate the potential for tremendous opportunity.

I am grateful for the faithful saints I have had the privilege of serving and working with over the years: the youth volunteers, the people who donate, sort, serve, and deliver food, acolytes, altar guild, flower guild, ushers, vestry members, homeless shelter volunteers, children's Sunday school teachers, counselors, spiritual directors, lay eucharistic visitors, pastoral care teams, mentors, and so many more. Community is cultivated through the faithful and reliable presence of those who give and serve, and lives are transformed when people are willing to show up and be a part of the movement of God in the world.

And also to you, the reader! Thank you! Thank you for showing up to learn and grow as Christians exploring life in the way of Jesus. Thank you for your faithfulness to God, your families, and your communities of faith.

Showing up can be very simple, but it can also be difficult to actually do. A variety of things can distract or lead us astray. However, Saint Matthias is our reminder to show up and strive toward reliability and faithfulness in our presence and witness.

The Feast of Saint Matthias does not offer anything flashy or fancy. It is a simple reminder: show up, be present.

Respond

The Bible tells us that the disciples "cast lots" to choose between Matthias and Justus. Did they roll the dice, toss a coin, or draw straws? We don't know exactly how they cast lots, but this process happens in other important times in scripture. In Leviticus, the method is used to separate the scapegoat from the goat being sacrificed. In the book of Numbers, it's used to divide the Promised Land among the Israelites. Even the sailors on Jonah's boat cast lots to figure out who was responsible for the storm at sea. In I Chronicles, lots are used to determine who was to receive which temple service. We are probably most familiar with this practice when the soldiers cast lots for Jesus' clothing during the crucifixion.

How do you cast lots? Do you ever close your eyes and pick something without peeking? Play rock, paper, scissors? Pick a number between 1 and 10?

Play a few games of rock, paper, scissors. Then talk about whether casting lots is a game of pure chance or guided by God.

Throughout the Bible, we see people of faith casting lots as outward and visible signs of God's will. Casting lots was sacramental. Today people are quick to attribute things to luck, chance, or coincidence, but perhaps it's God's hand at work.

Learn More

In the nine days of waiting between Jesus' Ascension and the Day of Pentecost, the disciples remained together in prayer. During this time, Peter reminded them that the defection and death of Judas had left the fellowship of the Twelve with a vacancy. The Acts of the Apostles records Peter's proposal that "one of the men who have accompanied us during all the time that the Lord Jesus went in and out among us, beginning from the baptism of John until the day when he was taken up from us—one of these men must become with us a witness to his resurrection" (Acts 1:21-22). Two men were nominated, Joseph called Barsabbas who was surnamed Justus, and Matthias. After prayer, the disciples cast lots, and the lot fell to Matthias, who was then enrolled with the eleven.

Scripture does not relate anything further about Matthias but gives him as an example to Christians of one whose faithful companionship with Jesus qualifies him to be a suitable witness to the resurrection and whose service is unheralded and unsung.

There are, however, several non-biblical early Christian accounts of his mission and ministry, such as the second-century text The Acts of Andrew and Matthias in Cannibal City. According to this account, immediately after the selection of Matthias, the apostles cast lots to determine which of them would take responsibility for which part of the world, and the unlucky Matthias was dispatched to a city of cannibals! Although an unabashedly fictionalized account, it is nevertheless an inspiring tale that shows Matthias being dealt the worst possible lot, and yet nevertheless responding to his call with equanimity, competence, and grace, which are the same qualities we see reflected in the canonical account that is given by scripture.

Pray

Almighty God, who in the place of Judas chose your faithful servant Matthias to be numbered among the Twelve: Grant that your Church, being delivered from false apostles, may always be guided and governed by faithful and true pastors; through Jesus Christ our Lord, who lives and reigns with you, in the unity of the Holy Spirit, one God, now and for ever. *Amen.*

Saint Joseph

Read

Psalm 89:1-29 *or* 89:1-4, 26-29 | 2 Samuel 7:4, 8-16
Romans 4:13-18 | Luke 2:41-52

Reflect

When we put our home on the market in preparation to move to seminary, someone suggested burying a miniature statue of Saint Joseph in our front yard. They promised it would help our home sell. I was more than a bit skeptical, to be honest. Nonetheless, I went to a Catholic bookstore and bought a boxed "Saint Joseph Home Selling Kit."

As we unboxed Saint Joseph and read the directions, I laughed at the fact we were to bury Saint Joseph upside down and facing the home.

Upside down. Seriously? Poor Joseph! What did he do to deserve this treatment?! But the directions

Author

Dorian Del Priore is an Episcopal priest who has been involved in youth ministry for more than twenty years. Dorian is a husband to Lauren and a father to Jordan and Brynn, and they live in Columbia, South Carolina.

said to bury the poor guy upside down, so that's what we did. Plunk. I felt bad for Joseph.

The truth is, though, we often find Saint Joseph in upside-down situations in the gospel stories, particularly in Matthew. Joseph learns his wife-to-be is pregnant, and then an angel comes to him in a dream, encouraging Joseph to embrace the mystery of the Holy Spirit and the revelation of this baby to be named Jesus. Faithfully, Joseph obeys the command from the angel of the Lord. Two more times, Joseph is visited by an angel in a dream: once, to flee to Egypt from Herod's violence, and then later to return from Egypt once things have settled down a bit.

I understand sleepless nights as a parent. Throw in a few angels visiting you between some tossing and turning, and I imagine life begins to feel surreal and topsy-turvy. But truth be told, it doesn't take an angel directing us to pick up and run to feel like life is upside down.

Parenting and family life comes at us with all sorts of curveballs and off-speed pitches. Late-night emergency room visits, bad grades, a lost stuffed animal, a terrifying diagnosis, job transitions, puberty, forgetting to swap a dollar for that tooth under the pillow, and a host of other scenarios turn life upside down. From momentary, mild situations to severe and trying scenarios, it is common to find ourselves upside down in a hole. Sometimes that hole is like an inconvenient pothole, and other times that hole is deep and dark.

What I find cool about Joseph is that, in the midst of these upside-down situations, he is portrayed as someone who is steadfast and faithful to both God and his family. He is open to mystery and willing to trust God. He nurtures and protects with compassion and humility. Further, he is venerated for being patient, persistent, courageous, and hard-working.

My dad happens to be a carpenter. He's one of those old-world carpenters with tough, calloused hands from years of hard labor. And he is also a gentle and humble man who joyfully paints his granddaughter's nails whenever she asks. He has never met a stranger and is generous to a fault. And when life turns upside down, he taught me to roll with the punches, get back up, and put one foot in front of the other.

Perseverance. Persistence. Courage. When I think of Joseph, it is easy to envision someone very much like my dad, which in turn makes it more accessible to become and embody a saint who feels so familiar. I find comfort and strength in the example of Joseph in the gospel stories because they tell of a man that feels mysteriously familiar to me.

When life hits hard and I find myself upside down and in a hole, I hope to respond in a manner befitting of Saint Joseph. I hope to provide for my family (and myself!) a sense of peace and a steadfast grounding of trust in God. I hope I can embrace the mystery that comes with the movement of God. Mostly, I hope to be steadfast and faithful to God and my family, especially when that hole is deep and dark.

Respond

Joseph was a carpenter. Honor his profession with some woodworking. Pull out the hammer and nails and some pieces of leftover lumber or gather some wood from your yard or park. Be creative about what you might make: since it's spring, a simple bird feeder might be a fun idea. If having a hammer is not age-appropriate, make cookies in the shape of carpenter's tools or even make a gingerbread tool box for Joseph (catholiccuisine.blogspot.com).

Learn More

In the face of circumstances that distressed even a man of such tenderness and obedience to God as Joseph, he accepted the vocation of protecting Mary and being a father to Jesus. He is honored in Christian tradition for the nurturing care and protection he provided for the infant Jesus and his mother in taking them to Egypt to escape Herod's slaughter of the innocents, and in rearing him as a faithful Jew at Nazareth.

The Gospel according to Matthew pictures Joseph as a man of deep devotion, open to mystical experiences, and as a man of compassion, who accepted his God-given responsibility with gentleness and humility. Joseph was a pious Jew, a descendant of David, and a carpenter by trade. As Joseph the Carpenter, he is considered the patron saint of the working man, one who not only worked with his hands, but taught his trade to Jesus. The little that is told of him is a testimony to the trust in God which values simple everyday duties, and gives an example of a loving husband and father.

Pray

O God, who from the family of your servant David raised up Joseph to be the guardian of your incarnate Son and the spouse of his virgin mother: Give us grace to imitate his uprightness of life and his obedience to your commands; through Jesus Christ our Lord, who lives and reigns with you and the Holy Spirit, one God, for ever and ever. *Amen.*

The Annunciation of Our Lord
Jesus Christ to the Blessed Virgin Mary

Read

Psalm 45 *or* 40:5-10 *or* Canticle 3 *or* 15
Isaiah 7:10-14 | Hebrews 10:4-10 | Luke 1:26-38

Reflect

"Greetings, you who are highly favored! The Lord is with you!"

If you're anything like me, you might have found scraps of Christmas lying around when you were getting ready to help your children with a school Valentine's Day celebration. It's still cold in most parts of the country, and we might still feel a bit of a holiday hangover when we're not quite sure what to do with ourselves in the days following the Feast of the Epiphany.

Author

Carrie Willard lives in Houston, Texas, with her husband, two sons, three dogs, and a cat who showed up on her front step one day.

Is it spring break?
When is Easter this year?
What is going on with Ash Wednesday?
Do we have enough king cake?

Forward Movement Collections   57

And the Feast of the Annunciation just shows up like the angel Gabriel, ready to disrupt our Easter Bunny browsing reverie at local store. We just got the Christmas tunes out of our heads, and now we're humming again, "Most Highly Favored Lady… Gloooooooria." This is the feast when we remember and celebrate Gabriel's announcement to Mary that she would be the mother of Jesus. It must have felt very disruptive.

Babies can do that to us.

When I became pregnant with our oldest child, I had experienced a series of miscarriages in the previous months, and my husband and I had just moved cross-country to Minnesota from Virginia. I was in a car accident, and our beloved dog was diagnosed with an autoimmune disorder. Our lives felt a little bit upside down. As a distraction from our topsy-turvy lives, we went to a live performance of "A Prairie Home Companion," which seemed like a very Minnesota thing to do. Throughout the first act of the performance, I could have sworn that everyone in the audience, but *especially* the guy sitting next to me, had bathed in beer before they arrived. The whole venue smelled like a brewery to me. During the intermission, my husband found a mostly empty beer can under my seat and disposed of it in the lobby, and with it, the beer smell disappeared.

On our way home that night, my husband said to me, "I don't care what those home pregnancy tests say or don't say. You're going to have a baby." Sure enough, nine months later and in the cold of a Minnesota winter, our baby arrived. (At eleven years old, he still doesn't like bad smells.)

Growing Christians

Our second child was a bit more of a tease. The blood tests that my doctor ordered to confirm my pregnancy with him were not showing the predicted results, which shows that you really can (despite the saying) be "a little bit pregnant." He came into the world with great drama—water breaking, cord wrapped around his neck twice, and weighing in at nine pounds, nine ounces. He followed that up by treating the whole family to a few months of colic. When strangers commented on his big, beautiful eyes, his older brother would tell them, "It's because he's nocturnal." I really only felt "highly favored" when he learned to sleep through the night.

YouTube is full of pregnancy announcements that are more glamorous than my beer can story or my wonky blood test results and less exotic than an angel's announcement. At some point, all of us were announced to our own mothers in some way. Even when that announcement is expected, even anticipated, it can be surprising to the person receiving it.

When we remember the Feast of the Annunciation, we think about how jarring it must have been to Mary. We also remember that Christmas feels like a long time from now, reminding us that Mary lived with the news of Jesus in her heart—and in her body—for a long time. Anybody who has waited for a baby, either through pregnancy or adoption, can tell you how long nine months can feel. The uncertainty in Mary's future must have made everything feel a bit more heavy. The Annunciation was just the beginning of the very real journey that she accepted to bring God's son into the world.

As Christians, we celebrate with Mary the surprising and disrupting news that Gabriel gave to her. We honor her as the highly favored one who received this news with grace. And we give thanks to her for bringing God's son into this world to save us all.

Respond

This is the day that Mary learned she would be a mother. Draw or write a Mother's Day card for Mary. Imagine that you are Jesus giving the card to his mother. What do you think Jesus would say? Also, take some time to make or write a card to your own mother or to someone who has mothered you in a wonderful way, regardless of your age (and hers)! Go ahead and give (or send) it as a surprise—and an early Mother's Day gift from the heart.

Learn More

Today's feast commemorates how God made known to a young Jewish woman that she was to be the mother of his Son. The Annunciation has been a major theme in Christian art, in both East and West, and innumerable sermons and poems have been composed about it. The term coined by Cyril of Alexandria for the Blessed Virgin, Theotokos ("the God-bearer"), was affirmed by the General Council of Ephesus in 431.

Many theologians stress that Mary accepted her vocation with perfect conformity of will. Mary's self-offering in response to God's call has been compared to that of Abraham, the father of believers. Just as Abraham was called to be the father of the chosen people, and accepted his call, so Mary was called to be the mother of the faithful, the new Israel. She is God's human agent in the mystery of the Incarnation. Her response to the angel, "Let it be to me according to your word," is identical with the faith expressed in the prayer that Jesus taught: "Your will be done on earth as in heaven."

But while many Christians emphasize the submissiveness of Mary, according to the sixth-century Syriac writer Jacob of Sarug, the most important words that Mary spoke were not those of quiet acquiescence but rather, "How can this be?" Indeed, in Jacob's account of the gospel encounter, Mary's response is much more than a single question. Instead, a teenage girl takes on an archangel in a theological debate and freely consents only when she has been convinced that the angel's word is true. In this interpretation, it is Mary's eagerness to understand God's plan and her own role in it that makes her exemplary rather than her meek consent. Jacob contrasts her behavior with Eve, who did not question the serpent that tempted her in the garden but uncritically accepted the claim that she and Adam would become like gods without testing it first. In Eve's case, "lack of doubt gave birth to death" because she simply believed whatever she was told and "was won over without any debate."

In both of these interpretations, however, our salvation is only possible because of Mary's free cooperation with God in that salvation. It has been said, "God made us without us, and redeemed us without us, but cannot save us without us." Mary's assent to God's call opened the way for God to accomplish the salvation of the world. It is for this reason that all generations have called her "blessed."

Pray

Pour your grace into our hearts, O Lord, that we who have known the incarnation of your Son Jesus Christ, announced by an angel to the Virgin Mary, may by his cross and passion be brought to the glory of his resurrection; who lives and reigns with you, in the unity of the Holy Spirit, one God, now and for ever. *Amen.*

Read

Psalm 31:9-16 | Isaiah 50:4-9a | Philippians 2:5-11
Matthew 26:14—27:66 *or* 27:11-54 (Year A)

Psalm 31:9-16 | Isaiah 50:4-9a | Philippians 2:5-11
Mark 14:1—15:47 *or* 15:1-39,(40-47) (Year B)

Psalm 31:9-16 | Isaiah 50:4-9a | Philippians 2:5-11
Luke 22:14—23:56 or 23:1-49

Reflect

Getting ready for Holy Week, I'm struck, as always, by how jarring the Palm Sunday liturgy is. One minute we're all shouting, "Hosanna, hosanna!" (Greek for 'save us'), and then the next thing we know, we're shouting "Crucify him." It's emotionally wrenching; hope and expectation give way to fury and fear. No settling in, no probing depths. Our liturgy moves us from place to place, scarcely able

Author

Sara Irwin, an Episcopal priest, is mother to Isaiah and Adah, and spouse to Noah Evans; they live near Pittsburgh, Pennsylvania. She loves tattoos, hiking, and making beer.

to take a breath. Why not split them up and leave space for the wideness of human experience? The crucifixion happens days after Jesus is welcomed into Jerusalem with branches and celebration, but Palm Sunday moves you faster than you can feel. The excitement of the crowd! The awkwardness of a procession! The intrigue of a trial, the panic and violence of a mob. Then, death and a terrible silence.

There's always an artificiality in liturgical life. I don't mean that it's false but just that the deep truths of human experience don't always slot neatly into whatever happens to be going on in the church year. People die tragic deaths on Christmas while we celebrate God's incarnation in human flesh. Even as we lament our sin and mourn, babies still get born during Lent. The despair or joy we feel in our own lives doesn't change because it's the "wrong" season. But Palm Sunday is something different—its breakneck speed leaves little room for our understanding to unfold. It's all movement, with no time to feel our way forward.

Know what else doesn't leave any space for taking a minute to settle in and feel a feeling?

Parenting.

As a parent of a nine- and twelve-year-old, one minute, I'm in the most ecstatic flow of meaningful conversation. We might be talking about bullying, or what we'll have for dinner, or the life cycle of a fruit fly. But the next minute, it's like a car crash. No one is quite sure what happened, but we definitely need some first responders over here to make sure that nobody loses a limb. Their worlds move so quickly, and the stakes are so high, they can't catch up. When my children were younger, the wild emotional swinging was also my own—one minute I was amazed by beauty, mystery, and holiness, the next bored out of my mind and thinking I'd sell a kidney for a nap.

This is where Palm Sunday is so helpful. Palm Sunday is a template for the glory of the whole gory mess; we are delighted and despondent, guilty and forgiven. We don't have to have it all mapped out and analyzed. This strange day of liturgy gives us a chance to see the flash of transcendence in all of it. Nobody at church on Palm Sunday has any illusion that either we as individuals or humanity as a whole have anything figured out. It's piecemeal, making meaning from moment to moment, seeing where it connects. The only gift we have to bring on Palm Sunday is our attentiveness, and that is true of life itself, particularly life with children. We try to bulldoze our emotions into submission, looking for linearity when there is no such thing. With our lives, like with the wild liturgy of this week, we are embarking on a journey that only God can hold.

We, in turn, need to let God hold us.

Respond

Some of us will pick up blessed palms from a basket sitting outside our church doors, and others live in areas where palm trees grow. For those of us who don't fall into either category, the rubric for the Liturgy of the Palms in *The Book of Common Prayer* states, "the branches of palm or of other trees or shrubs to be carried in the procession may be distributed to the people." So go ahead, clip any branch or bush from your front yard or print and color a palm frond coloring page (illustratedministry.com). Wave them while walking around your home and shouting Hosanna!

Learn More

The pilgrim Egeria describes an observance of Palm Sunday in the late fourth century. Christians gathered on the other side of the Mount of Olives, in a place called Bethphage, where they read together the story of Jesus' entry into Jerusalem. They walked to the Mount of Olives and down the hillside into the city. Egeria tells us that these early Christians waved palm or olive tree branches, sang psalms (especially 118), and shouted the antiphon: "Blessed is he who comes in the name of the Lord!"

Our observance of Palm Sunday, nearly 2,000 years later, follows the same pattern. The service, found in the prayer book on pages 270-273, typically begins with the Liturgy of the Palms, which starts outdoors or in another place away from the church building. This part of the service commemorates the triumphal entry into Jerusalem, and the congregation re-enacts that story as a community, waving own palm branches while walking into the sanctuary, singing or saying hymns of praise and joy, including the refrain "Blessed is he who comes in the name of the Lord," and often Psalm 118, the very same words Egeria described as being said in the fourth century.

The service continues as usual until it is time for the gospel. *The Book of Common Prayer* calls this holy day "The Sunday of the Passion: Palm Sunday" because it is a day of remembrance not only of Jesus' triumphal entry into Jerusalem but also the rest of the passion narrative: Jesus' betrayal, trial, crucifixion, and death. So on Palm Sunday every year, the passion gospel is either read or chanted.

—*Walk in Love: Episcopal Beliefs & Practices*,
published by Forward Movement

Pray

Almighty and everliving God, in your tender love for the human race you sent your Son our Savior Jesus Christ to take upon him our nature, and to suffer death upon the cross, giving us the example of his great humility: Mercifully grant that we may walk in the way of his suffering, and also share in his resurrection; through Jesus Christ our Lord, who lives and reigns with you and the Holy Spirit, one God, for ever and ever. *Amen.*

—*The Book of Common Prayer*

MAUNDY THURSDAY

This date changes each year.
Check your calendar to determine the date.

Read

Psalm 116:1, 10-17 | Exodus 12:1-4, (5-10), 11-14
1 Corinthians 11:23-26 | John 13:1-17, 31b-35

Reflect

I am currently on the twentieth day of being home with my husband, two small children, and my mother. When I agreed to write this post, I never imagined this would be our life heading into Holy Week. I jumped at the opportunity to write about Maundy Thursday—it is one of my favorite services in the church year. I planned to tell you stories about the incredible moments I shared washing the feet of acquaintances, friends, and strangers. I was convinced that after reading my post, you would put your family in the car and rush to the closest church—so compelling would my argument for this experience be.

Author

Meaghan Brower serves as executive director of the Episcopal Conference Center in Rhode Island and lives in Newport with Jonathan, a furniture maker, and their three children.

And yet, here we are, quarantined. There aren't any church doors open for you to walk through, untie your shoes, and then wash another person's feet. Given the sudden new landscape, I found myself returning to the drawing board for this post. While my past experiences stand as having been deeply moving and profound, those stories seemed less relevant. I had to consider what Maundy Thursday could and would look like for us this year.

Thankfully, I have an understanding husband and mother and children so small they have no sense of the calendar. So we decided to move Maundy Thursday up a week. I wanted to see what it would be like if we shared a family meal, took off our shoes and socks, and washed each other's feet in our dining room. I wanted to try it, so I could tell you about it.

When I made the decision to test run Maundy Thursday, I wondered how our family would feel by the time we observed it. Will we want anything to do with one another? Will we even be able to make conversation at dinner without pulling out our hair due to the repetition of all our family dynamics?

What I didn't expect was that I would wake up the morning of our dinner awash in grief. Grief has been with us in one form or another since this started, but on this day it was particularly heavy. Maybe it was the fact that the sky was gray again. Maybe it was because I knew I had a staff meeting ahead of me in which we would need to make tough decisions. Maybe it was because my oldest son asked to come home, and I knew he would have to quarantine for two weeks upon return. There were plenty of reasons, but the fact remains I woke up feeling heavy. I moved through the day on the verge of tears, and I looked toward my evening plans with fatigue. I didn't want a special meal. I didn't want to convince two children to wash each other's feet. I didn't want extra work to have still another family meal.

Interestingly, the word maundy comes from the word mandate, as it serves as a reminder of the actions Jesus mandated us to do before his death. If I'm honest, Jesus' mandate might not have been enough to make dinner happen, but a writing deadline and my own expectations did the trick. I was (self) mandated, and so I did it.

At lunch, we told the kids about our "special" dinner. My son Sam (age five) immediately insisted he didn't want to wash feet or have his feet washed. I had promised myself that this activity would be encouraged, but not forced, so we made an agreement that he could take pictures.

Mid-afternoon, I stopped everything I was trying to get done during the day to set the table and start making it look special for the family. I was surprised to find myself warming to the task.

Then I put some work into the area where we would wash one another's feet. My children are short, so this required some creativity.

Thankfully, a meal on Maundy Thursday typically calls for simplicity, so I prepped soup and grilled cheese sandwiches. And then, even though every part of me didn't want to do it,

I left the house for the walk I take every day at 4 p.m. It was raining, and I'm tired of walking the same three routes. But I did it anyway, and the fresh air helped. By the time I got home, I was almost looking forward to dinner.

I finished cooking, and we gathered at the table. We used a simple service. We lit candles and prayed, and suddenly Sam realized he wasn't dressed in fancy clothes for our special dinner. He left the table to go change. My husband looked at me, waiting for me to insist he stay at the table, but that wasn't the deal. We let him go.

We ate, shared stories from scripture, and talked about why Jesus washed the feet of his friends. My kids mostly listened and mostly stayed at the table— a victory. By the end of the meal, they were excited for the next part and began asking, "Is it time?"

We moved to the bench, and Sam started taking pictures. He was clear that he wanted pictures of everybody's feet. Including the dog (whose feet we did not wash).

We asked who wanted to go first. Sam did, of course. Kids, man. Then we took turns, each person choosing who would go next and who would wash that person's feet. When our three-year-old daughter said she wanted to wash my feet, I sat on the bench and put my feet in the bowl. I looked down as her sweet hands patted the water over my feet—no inhibition, all tenderness. My heart caught in my throat. We watched one another take turns, and it was so very beautiful. For a few fleeting minutes, we shared sacred time, a total departure from all the other shared experiences over the last three weeks. In this moment, time stood still in the best possible way.

In the end, my message about Maundy Thursday is the same as it would have been had I written the reflection before ever considering what "social distancing" meant. And here is the message: kneeling at the feet of another human and washing their feet is one of the most profound, beautiful, and sacred moments I have been privileged to share in my life.

Every. Single. Time.

I knew that to be true from years of washing the feet of parishioners, friends, and strangers, and now I know it to be true with the people I am the most intimate with and yet with whom I never think to kneel down before to honor as Jesus honored his friends.

There's a chance I will look back over this time with my family and remember this meal and foot washing as the single most precious moment we shared together during the shocking, unprecedented, and outrageous spring of 2020.

Listen friends: you likely won't want to do this. You'll wake up and want to take the easy road—there's no priest to notice if you're observing Maundy Thursday, no obligation, no altar guild commitment. You'll be so tired of your family that you'll rather eat dinner with *anyone* else. But I promise you—Jesus will be present with you. And you will be so very grateful to have encountered him in the faces of your family.

Respond

Consider inviting your entire household to thoughtfully prepare, eat, and conclude a meal together in a way that honors Jesus' last supper with his friends. Once the meal is over and feet have been washed, plan to strip the kitchen table and scrub it. This mirrors what happens with the altar at church, where the symbols of worship are removed as we await the crucifixion. Perhaps your table is serving as workspace or school desk or the hub for mail and other drop-off items. The kitchen table often works overtime, and stripping it of signs of life can be a powerful symbol of these holy days. The challenge may be in leaving it barren until Easter morning, but doing so offers a reminder of the tomb.

Learn More

On Maundy Thursday, we remember Jesus' final meal with his friends before he was crucified; this is often called the Last Supper. In a sense, Christians recall this event every week with the celebration of Holy Communion. But Maundy Thursday offers a special commemoration of this meal, following the service in *The Book of Common Prayer* on pages 274-275 or *The Book of Occasional Services*, pages 93-94.

The word maundy comes from the Latin word for commandment, because Maundy Thursday is a day for remembering Jesus' commandments. Matthew, Mark, and Luke all tell similar stories of what Jesus did on that night, while the Gospel of John tells another story and introduces another commandment. John's version of the Last Supper doesn't talk about the bread and wine. Instead Jesus kneels on the floor and washes his disciples' feet in an example of servanthood.

In many congregations, the Maundy Thursday service continues after the readings and sermon with a ceremony of the washing of feet. Sometimes this is done symbolically: the clergy or other members of leadership wash the feet of a specific number of people (usually twelve), or the clergy wash everyone's feet. But perhaps more appropriately the foot washing should be done by everyone—everyone both washing and getting washed—so that all are participating in and fulfilling Christ's commandment: "So if I, your Lord and Teacher, have washed your feet, you also ought to wash one another's feet" (John 13:14).

After the ceremony of washing of feet, the service continues with the Prayers of the People and then Holy Communion. This is the last celebration of Holy Eucharist until the Great Vigil of Easter. Some churches choose to consecrate more bread and wine than is necessary at this service in order to reserve some of the sacrament for Good Friday. If additional elements are being reserved, they are taken, often by a solemn procession, to a separate chapel or other place out of the main sanctuary. The area where the sacrament is kept is called the Altar of Repose. In some congregations, people remain through the night to pray and keep vigil with the sacrament, as an echo of the disciples who Jesus asked to stay awake and pray with him in the Garden of Gethsemane.

After Holy Communion is concluded, many communities observe the custom of stripping the altar. Members of the congregation remove all decoration and ornaments from the church and veil or cover all visible crosses. This can be done in silence or with a recitation of Psalm 22. As the sanctuaries are stripped of their decorations, it is a reminder of the moment in the passion story when Jesus is stripped of his clothes. Many communities conclude by washing the altar and extinguishing the sanctuary lamp, the sign of Christ's continued presence.

After the altar is stripped, the ministers and people depart in silence. There is no dismissal or end to the service. This silence invites people to remember that the Triduum services are part and parcel of one another—they are one continuous liturgy telling one continuous story. Maundy Thursday is the first act of the Triduum; the story continues with our remembering the next day with Good Friday and on Saturday night or Sunday morning with the Easter Vigil.

—*Walk in Love: Episcopal Beliefs & Practices*,
published by Forward Movement

Pray

Almighty Father, whose dear Son, on the night before he suffered, instituted the Sacrament of his Body and Blood: Mercifully grant that we may receive it thankfully in remembrance of Jesus Christ our Lord, who in these holy mysteries gives us a pledge of eternal life; and who now lives and reigns with you and the Holy Spirit, one God, for ever and ever. *Amen.*

—*The Book of Common Prayer*

GOOD FRIDAY

*This date changes each year.
Check your calendar to
determine the date.

Read

Psalm 22 | Isaiah 52:13—53:12
Hebrews 10:16-25 *or* 4:14-16; 5:7-9 | John 18:1—19:42

Reflect

I was baptized at the Easter Vigil liturgy at St. Martin-in-the-Field's Episcopal Church in Columbia, South Carolina, when

Author

Dorian Del Priore is an Episcopal priest who has been involved in youth ministry for more than twenty years. Dorian is a husband to Lauren and a father to Jordan and Brynn, and they live in Columbia, South Carolina.

I was seventeen years old. As part of my preparation, I remember the rector suggesting that I attend and participate in all the Holy Week liturgies they offered. Looking back thirty-two years, I'll be honest: I don't remember anything particular about the Good Friday service. But I do believe the fullness of those experiences that week rooted in me a love for how we tell and live into the passion narrative through our liturgy.

We have tried to cultivate in our own family both the importance of Holy Week and a love for the experiences that come with it. The Maundy Thursday foot washing is a family favorite, particularly for my son and how it connects with his experiences at our diocesan "Happening" retreat, which includes a powerful foot washing liturgy. Using that as leverage, there is a built-in teaching moment that Maundy Thursday is just a portion of the Triduum and thus intimately connected with Good Friday (and ultimately Easter).

The death of Jesus is not an easy topic to discuss with children, and many have anxiety about such a conversation. At my previous parish, St. Peter's in Greenville, South Carolina, we offered an interactive Stations of the Cross liturgy on Good Friday: the Way of the Cross for Children and Families. Adapted from the "Way of the Cross" in the *Book of Occasional Services*, my friend and mentor, the Rev. Furman Buchanan, developed this simple, beautiful, and age-appropriate liturgy for children and families to engage the drama of Christ's passion and death. Of course, folks of all ages were welcome to attend—and many did.

Our adapted Way of the Cross includes an opening devotion and eight stations. We gather at the front of the church, and the stations are set up around the church grounds so that we journey together to each station. It is very much a pilgrimage experience.

Middle and high school youth lead the stations, reading reflections and helping facilitate the interactive portion of their station. The stations engage the senses: they touch a crown of thorns, the group carries a large cross together, they hear women weeping and grieving for Jesus, taste vinegar (sour wine) with bread, receive a nail, hear a large bell toll to signify the death of Jesus, and then finally the kids help roll a large cardboard stone in front of a big refrigerator-box tomb.

Music is an important facet of the Way of the Cross. It opens, closes, and provides the connectivity during the movement between stations. Songs and hymns have been sung *a cappella*, and guitars have been used for accompaniment.

We open with something familiar for the younger children, like "Jesus Loves the Little Children." The traveling music has most often been "Kum Ba Yah." It is familiar, easy for little kids, and repetitive. Many other Taizé or children's songs would work as long as there is a sense of reverence. The closing hymn is #172 in the 1982 Hymnal (verses 1 & 4): "Were you there when they crucified my Lord?" Afterward, we gather for a light reception, offering space and time to answer questions and reflect on what was experienced.

I truly believe this liturgy has been an experience that provides entry points for parents to discuss the more difficult realities of Good Friday with their children. Instead of focusing too much on the details of what Jesus experienced, I shift the conversation to the ways in which Good Friday displays how God in Christ relates to humans in and through suffering. Further, one can make the explicit connection to the annunciation, the nativity story, and Jesus being named Emmanuel, God with us.

I ask kids what the word suffering means to them, bringing it to their level, and they usually talk about fear, illness, and those sorts of themes. We know God loves us and cares for us because of what God in Christ experienced on Good Friday.

Another point I have made with my children is that we experience Good Friday through the lens of Easter and how this impacts the way we see death. Our burial liturgies hold the tension between joy and grief. We find joy as we celebrate our love for that person and joy in God's promise that we will never be separated from the love of God. There's grief in our sorrow as we are parted by death from those we love. This is the reality we experience for Jesus on Good Friday. While we don't want to look too quickly toward Easter, I believe keeping the lens broader is more appropriate and helpful for children and many youth.

I tell my children and the young people I work with: even on the darkest of days, we still believe that the sun will rise again. Even in the most desolate and bleak of circumstances, we always have hope. This is the gift of Good Friday.

Respond

There are many Stations of the Cross liturgies available online. Do an online search or try the audio versions created by St. John's Cathedral in Denver, Colorado, which includes images, prayers, and a brief audio reflection for each station, and Episcopal Migration Ministries, which includes a meditation and petition for each station.

Learn More

Good Friday is the day when Christians recall with prayers and readings the crucifixion of the Lord and Savior on the cross. On this day, the people and ministers enter in silence into a church that is bare of ornamentation following the stripping of the altar on Maundy Thursday. The liturgy on this day, like the church, is "stripped down" to the essentials; it is brief and solemn.

The prayer book service (pages 276-282) begins with an opening collect (prayer) and readings. Then, just as on Palm Sunday, there is a reading of the passion, this time from the Gospel of John. After the passion is a sermon and an optional hymn. Then the congregation engages in an extended time of prayer, using the ancient tradition of the solemn collects. These prayers are a reminder that on Good Friday, Christians do not merely focus on their own grief or sense of loss at the death of Jesus but instead allow that grief to fuel prayers and actions on behalf of the whole world.

The service of Good Friday can end here, with a hymn, the Lord's Prayer, or a final prayer. But *The Book of Common Prayer* also includes two additional, optional parts of the service: Veneration of the Cross and Holy Communion from the reserved sacrament.

For Veneration of the Cross, a wooden cross is brought into the church and placed in the sight of the people. The prayer book includes the words to appropriate anthems that can be sung or said, or the congregation can choose another suitable anthem.

Growing Christians

During or after the anthems, people can offer "appropriate devotions" to the cross. In some communities people kneel before the cross in prayer. Some might choose to touch or kiss the cross, as a sign of devotion. In other communities, people lay flowers at the foot of the cross, similar to how we might put flowers on a grave at a funeral. All of these options are different ways that communities attempt to honor the holy cross of Jesus, by which our Savior redeemed the world.

The final option for the Good Friday service is to celebrate Holy Communion—but in an unusual manner. Tradition demands that priests do not consecrate the bread and wine on Good Friday as a way of remembering that Jesus was dead, in the grave, absent from presence on this day. Using the bread and wine set in reserve on Maundy Thursday, the minister conducts a simple service of communion, offering the bread and wine without the traditional prayer of consecration. The community eats and drinks all of the bread and wine that remains so that there is no sacrament until the bread and wine are consecrated for the first time at Easter.

The Good Friday service concludes with a simple prayer, no blessing or dismissal, and the people depart in silence. Good Friday is the second act of the Triduum, which will continue and conclude with the Great Vigil of Easter.

—*Walk in Love: Episcopal Beliefs & Practices*,
published by Forward Movement

Pray

Almighty God, we pray you graciously to behold this your family, for whom our Lord Jesus Christ was willing to be betrayed, and given into the hands of sinners, and to suffer death upon the cross; who now lives and reigns with you and the Holy Spirit, one God, for ever and ever. *Amen.*

—*The Book of Common Prayer*

Holy Saturday

*This date changes each year.
Check your calendar to determine the date.*

Read

Psalm 31:1-4, 15-16 | Job 14:1-14 *or*
Lamentations 3:1-9, 19-24 |1 Peter 4:1-8
Matthew 27:57-66 *or* John 19:38-42

Reflect

If anyone is to feast on Easter Sunday, food must be prepared.

If food is to be prepared for Easter Sunday, work must be done on Holy Saturday.

Or maybe you are better at planning ahead than I am!

I remember many Holy Saturdays when I thought wistfully of the words, "On the Sabbath they rested according to the commandment" (Luke 23:56).

Since I became a mother, I have never rested on Holy Saturday. On the other hand, Saturday is not my

Author

Nurya Love Parish is an Episcopal priest and ministry developer and was the founding editor of Grow Christians. She has reached the late teenage stage of parenting with her firefighter husband, and they live in Rockford, Michigan.

Forward Movement Collections

Sabbath. And I usually rest on Easter Sunday or during Easter Week at some point, so it all works out.

This year, our traditions are going by the wayside as some members of our extended family travel for a funeral taking place on Holy Saturday. Our Easter Sunday will be very unusual this year.

But Easter lasts for fifty days! And it would not be the same without hot cross buns. So this Holy Saturday, I'm making them even though not everyone will be here to eat them on Easter Sunday.

Today is a day for waiting and for preparing. It is a day of anticipation. We wait with hope.

Unlike the women who rested in observance of the commandment, we know what comes next in this story.

We are blessed to be preparing for a celebration.

Respond

Plan an at-home Easter vigil. Search online or visit GrowChristians.org/holydays. The Grow Christians resource is an ideal length for young children with only three readings selected. The authors even include "I wonder" questions for each story that will feel familiar to children who are missing their Godly Play formation classes. Emily Given, Erika Bower, and Michael Smith of St. Thomas Episcopal Church in Whitemarsh, Pennsylvania, created a list of activities for each day of Holy Week, including activities for an at-home vigil. The suggestions are practical, doable, and theologically sound.

Learn More

Consisting of only one page (283) in *The Book of Common Prayer*, the service for Holy Saturday is simple and brief. There is no celebration of Holy Eucharist on this day, a stark reminder that Jesus is absent, dead and in the tomb. Instead, the service consists of a collect, a few readings, and a short anthem from the Burial Office (pages 484 or 492). The liturgy offers no easy answers or trite statements. The mood of the day is quiet and still, reflective of an old tradition that required silence throughout the day.

The Great Vigil of Easter is the fullest expression of Christian life and joy in the earthly pilgrimage. On this night, Christians enter into the heart of their faith. Starting on page 285 of the prayer book, the service begins in darkness, a reminder that what is to come emerges from the darkness of Good Friday and Holy Saturday, the cross and the grave. In the darkness, a fire is kindled. This recalls both the creation of light—the first creative act by God—and the light that is brought into the world in the new creation of Jesus Christ. The new fire lights the paschal candle, which stands as a symbol of Christ, both in its association with light and in the candle's association with baptism. The paschal candle is taken to the front of the sanctuary, where it will remain throughout the fifty days of Easter.

Next, a minister sings or says the *Exsultet*, an ancient hymn that proclaims the heart of Easter joy: "Rejoice and sing now, all the round earth, bright with glorious splendor, for darkness has been vanquished by our eternal King" (286). This hymn is a raucous celebration of the mighty power exhibited in the resurrection, when light overcame darkness, when love overcame sin, and when life overcame death. Again and again the *Exsultet* proclaims, "This is the night…", a reminder that in this holy moment, heaven is brought down to earth and the past is brought into the present as we celebrate our salvation as though it were the first time.

The service continues with a selection of stories from the Old Testament; at least two or as many as nine are read. The reading from Exodus, when God brings the people out of slavery in Egypt, is always read. The stories are a reminder of the whole arc of salvation, the way that God has been present with and loved humanity from the beginning of creation.

Following the readings is the service for Holy Baptism. The Great Vigil of Easter was once the main day for new Christians to be welcomed into the church through baptism, and it continues to be a major occasion for baptisms. If there are no candidates for Holy Baptism, those present instead renew their baptismal vows, recommitting themselves on this holy night to the life of faith.

Then Easter is joyously proclaimed with the words, "Alleluia. Christ is risen." The people respond, "The Lord is risen indeed. Alleluia" (294). This simple statement proclaims the deepest truth as Christians: the reality of the resurrection of Jesus Christ.

After joyfully proclaiming the resurrection of Jesus three times, the congregation sings one of the canticles of celebration. The service continues with an epistle reading, psalm, gospel reading, sermon, and prayers of the people. Then the table is set for the first eucharist of Easter, a true thanksgiving in which Christians recall with gladness Christ's resurrection and are nourished by Christ's Body and Blood to proclaim it to the world.

—*Walk in Love: Episcopal Beliefs & Practices*,
published by Forward Movement

Pray

O God, Creator of heaven and earth: Grant that, as the crucified body of your dear Son was laid in the tomb and rested on this holy Sabbath, so we may await with him the coming of the third day, and rise with him to newness of life; who now lives and reigns with you and the Holy Spirit, one God, for ever and ever. *Amen.*

—*The Book of Common Prayer*

Easter Day

This date changes each year.
Check your calendar to determine the date.

Read

Psalm 118:1-2, 14-24 | Acts 10:34-43 *or* Isaiah 25:6-9
1 Corinthians 15:1-11 *or* Acts 10:34-43
John 20:1-18 *or* Mark 16:1-8

Reflect

One weekend in February, just before Lent, we were outside doing some yard work. We have a little peach tree we planted when we moved into this house, one that last year was finally big enough to supply us with a cobbler's worth of peaches.

> **Author**
>
> **Heather Sleightholm** is an artist, wife, and mother living in northeastern Oklahoma.

Since late winter is the time to prune fruit trees, we were cutting off branches that were already swelling with buds. The kids and I decided to bring some of the branches inside to "force" into blooming, and there you have it—an Easter tree was born!

Placed in a large jar of water in the kitchen, those dormant branches slowly began to blossom and unfurl. We decorated them with little Easter eggs and enjoyed a magical early coming of spring as Lent began and the familiar story of resurrection and rebirth was told at church and in storybooks at home.

I had first heard about forcing tree blossoms in the sweet little book *A Time To Blossom* by Tovah Martin, which beautifully shares seasonal activities to do with children in the garden throughout the year.

Forcing blooming branches can be done with most types of flowering tree or shrub, such as apple, plum, cherry or pear trees. Other pretty flowering spring branches include forsythia and pussy willow, which you can usually find at the local grocery florist around early spring.

Palm Sunday saw palm fronds and crosses gathered up at church, slipped into pockets and purses, and brought home. I've been collecting icons for a few years now, and it's a routine for us now to place the palm crosses in behind the icons and take the old crosses from last year down to bury in the garden.

My youngest is two, and for him any excuse is a good excuse to dig in the dirt. And here's hoping that a little holy water infused palm works miracles for uninspired peonies!

These little moments with my children, forging new traditions and using the church year as a family rhythm, are so special to me—but they take practice. I didn't grow up practicing Lent— or Advent. Or know much about feast days or holy days. I am learning along with the kids, and it's been special for us all.

This year, to get us a little more into the Easter spirit, we decided to make a spring/Easter altar in our living room. As impressive as it may sound, it was just the top of a little dresser in our entryway.

The altar was inspired by the concept of seasonal altars used in Waldorf education, which also celebrates nature and the festivals of the year. We used things we had around the house to create our altar, and part of the fun was the gathering of the items. Some of the items we chose were favorite children's books (we used Tasha Tudor's *A Time to Keep,* which is a wonderful book about the celebrations of the year with a homespun flavor), stuffed animals, papier mâché eggs, laminated saint cards, wooden eggs, bowls and baskets, and a battery-operated candle.

In short, everything on our altar is child-friendly and able to survive little curious hands and capture a child's imagination. And not only is using items around the house inexpensive to do, but it also helped the kids look at things they already have with fresh eyes.

It was a lot of fun for us to create these little vignettes, and I imagine we will keep it up throughout the seasons. These projects are learning experiences for us all and are working themselves into the rhythm of our lives by bring the liturgical year out of the church and into our home.

Respond

Create a home altar. Take suggestions from the reflection and find items from around the house. To up the ante, challenge each other to find an item from a specific room (a kitchen item, something off the bookshelf, a stuffed animal, something from the backpack, etc.). As you're collecting the items and creating your home altar, ask each other questions (and listen carefully to the answers!).

What things in the toy box remind of us spring or Easter? Why? Where do we see the Easter story written or illustrated or referred to? What colors, objects, or tokens remind us of Easter?

Learn More

The Great Vigil of Easter was just the beginning; the celebration of Christ's resurrection continues in the rest of the services on Easter Day. Furthermore, the joy of Easter is so great that it cannot even be contained in one day. Easter Day is only the first day of the Easter Season, which begins the Great Fifty Days of Easter. The paschal candle remains lit and in the front of the church throughout the season, calling to mind the light of Christ that was proclaimed at the vigil and that continues to shine. Throughout the season of Easter, the service begins with the same proclamation of Christ's resurrection that we heard at the Great Vigil: "Alleluia. Christ is risen." In fact, additional alleluias are sprinkled throughout the service of

Holy Eucharist during the season of Easter: at the opening, during Holy Eucharist, and at the dismissal. Alleluia is a word of great celebration, a shout of unbridled joy. These extra alleluias are not added at other times of the year, so they serve as a way to set the Great Fifty Days of Easter above and apart as an occasion of deep joy.

—*Walk in Love: Episcopal Beliefs & Practices*,
published by Forward Movement

Pray

Almighty God, who through your only-begotten Son Jesus Christ overcame death and opened to us the gate of everlasting life: Grant that we, who celebrate with joy the day of the Lord's resurrection, may be raised from the death of sin by your life-giving Spirit; through Jesus Christ our Lord, who lives and reigns with you and the Holy Spirit, one God, now and for ever. *Amen.*

—*The Book of Common Prayer*

Saint Mark the Evangelist

Read

Psalm 2 *or* 2:7-10 | Isaiah 52:7-10
Ephesians 4:7-8, 11-16 | Mark 1:1-15 *or* 16:15-20

Reflect

Gilded chapels and stained-glass light have been the setting of my past reflections on the feast day of Saint Mark the Evangelist. But this year, there is COVID-19. It seems that nothing is left untouched by the pandemic. While this is a strange and unknown experience for us, it is not unknown to the church.

Held in this wider context and seeking insight for today, we remember Saint Mark and the writing attributed to him.

Mark's Gospel is *marked* by urgency. He employs the word "immediately" to push from scene to scene as he proclaims the good news of Jesus Christ and pushes all the way to the cliffhanger ending, "So they went out and fled

Author

Genevieve Razim, an Episcopal priest in Texas, has been married for twenty-five years and is the mother of two young men. Her favorite place to be is at the table with loved ones.

from the tomb, for terror and amazement had seized them; and they said nothing to anyone, for they were afraid." Mark tells the good news with urgency but then ends with witnesses paralyzed by fear.

Is this how it ends? (Yes, the original manuscript ends there!)

Clearly, the fearful witnesses—with God's grace—found their way forward to share the good news of Christ with others because…we are here!

Saint Mark earns his title "Evangelist," putting generation after generation on the spot, challenging them to share the good news in the midst of hardships, wars, and plagues. And because of their witness, we are here today.

Now Mark challenges us.

Are we willing to allow the good news to go untold?

How will we witness within our life circumstances?

How will fear be an obstacle for us, specifically during the COVID-19 pandemic?

For the poor, the imprisoned, the essential workers, the medical staff, and those with pre-existing medical conditions, fear is overt. For many sheltering-at-home with the family under one roof all day, fear can be covert. But fear is present: fear of suffering, hardship, and death.

If you are reading this post, it might be that your fears are hidden under a patchwork quilt of professional obligations, family activities, and a spectrum of connections and disconnections. Meeting (or missing) work or volunteer deadlines, learning to bake bread while children put clothes on the cat. Toddler meltdowns, bored but creative teenagers, sidewalk chalk drawings, and the never-ending loads of dishes and laundry. All stitched together by worry over health, political, and economic issues.

It is important to look under this patchwork quilt to acknowledge our fear. This can lead us to question how we are coping with it and consider how our conscious (or unconscious) coping strategies align with our faith and values. How do these behaviors affect those around me?

Author Brené Brown reminds us: "We don't have to be scary when we're scared." Positively managing our fear—through prayer, healthy lifestyle choices, generosity, and acts of kindness—is an opportunity to witness and share the good news. The young ones who tug on our sleeves and sit at our tables are watching us, learning what faith looks like in times of fear and crisis.

Saint Mark urgently shares the good news that life in Christ promises not a way *around* suffering, hardship, and death, but a way *through* it.

And though there may be moments in which we feel paralyzed by fear, just as our faith ancestors did, this will not be the end of the story. With God's grace, we too will find our way forward, as we seek to align our words and actions with our faith, day by day. And in the process, another generation will come to know and share "the good news of Jesus Christ, the Son of God" (Mark 1:1).

Respond

Turn your sidewalk or driveway into a work of art. Using chalk, create a stained-glass window or draw a bouquet of flowers. Create an obstacle course or hopscotch. Or write some encouraging messages that can be a blessing to passersby. You might also ask your church leadership if you can chalk the parking lot or sidewalks as another way of expressing God's love to your neighbors.

Learn More

A disciple of Jesus, named Mark, appears in several places in the New Testament. If all references to Mark can be accepted as referring to the same person, we learn that he was the son of a woman who owned a house in Jerusalem. Church tradition suggests that Mark may have been the young man who fled naked when Jesus was arrested in the Garden of Gethsemane. In his letter to the Colossians, Paul refers to "Mark the cousin of Barnabas," who was with him in his imprisonment. Mark set out with Paul and Barnabas on their first missionary journey, but he turned back for reasons which failed to satisfy Paul (Acts 15:36-40). When another journey was planned,

Paul refused to have Mark with him. Instead, Mark went with Barnabas to Cyprus. The breach between Paul and Mark was later healed, and Mark became one of Paul's companions in Rome, as well as a close friend of Peter's.

An early tradition recorded by Papias, Bishop of Hierapolis in Asia Minor at the beginning of the second century, names Mark as the author of the gospel bearing his name, drawing his information from the teachings of Peter. In his First Letter, Peter refers to "my son Mark," which shows a close relationship between the two men (1 Peter 5:13).

The Church of Alexandria in Egypt claimed Mark as its first bishop and most illustrious martyr, and the great Church of St. Mark in Venice commemorates the disciple who progressed from turning back while on a missionary journey with Paul and Barnabas to proclaiming in his gospel Jesus of Nazareth as Son of God, and bearing witness to that faith in his later life as friend and companion to the apostles Peter and Paul.

Pray

Almighty God, by the hand of Mark the evangelist you have given to your church the Gospel of Jesus Christ the Son of God: We thank you for this witness, and pray that we may be firmly grounded in its truth; through Jesus Christ our Lord, who lives and reigns with you and the Holy Spirit, one God, for ever and ever. *Amen.*

Saint Philip and Saint James, Apostles

Read

Psalm 119:33-40 | Isaiah 30:18-21
2 Corinthians 4:1-6 | John 14:6-14

Reflect

Today we celebrate the feast day of two of the twelve apostles, Philip and James. Philip and James are not the most well-known of Jesus' disciples. Philip is mentioned in two significant ways in the Bible: Jesus turns to him for help with the feeding of the 5,000, and at the Last Supper, Philip says, "Lord, show us the Father, and we will be satisfied." When you read about James, you find several references to others named James, and you learn that he's not the most important one. He's listed as one of the Twelve, and that's pretty much it.

Author

Miriam Willard McKenney finds extreme joy in parenting her three girls: Nia, Kaia, and Jaiya. She and her husband, David, met at the Union of Black Episcopalians conference in 1981.

So what can we learn from these two men? I found myself wishing I could find something amazing that they had said, something heroic they had done. Then I realized I was being terribly narrow-minded. We have lots to learn and celebrate about Phillip and James, and we don't need to know anything more about them than this: they walked away from everything they knew and everything they loved to follow Jesus. Can you imagine doing that? I can't.

They don't need to be extraordinary characters in the Jesus story. Philip and James teach us that if they can do it, we can too. I'm always looking for ways to empower my girls to know that they can be whoever and whatever they want to be, combined with a heavy dose of reality. We can't all be superstars. Everyone won't remember us or know our stories. But we can walk with Jesus, and we can follow his teachings to the best of our abilities. That makes us special.

Apostles were people who said yes when other people said no. The disciples unconsciously lived the parables Jesus told. Philip and James made the ultimate sacrifice and walked away from everything they knew and loved to follow someone they just met. Somehow, they knew that Jesus offered something they couldn't comprehend or deny. We would do well to teach our children to follow the example of the apostles, who followed and then risked their lives to share the good news with others.

Saint Philip and Saint James, thank you for saying yes to Jesus.

Respond

Celebrate this feast day with a feast. Saint Philip is often depicted with two loaves of bread, in reference to his response to Jesus and the feeding of the 5,000. Plus, he's also known as a patron saint of pastry chefs. If you're not in the mood for bread and pastries, consider some Greek food in honor of Saint Philip's role as intermediary for the Greeks who came to see Jesus.

Learn More

The two apostles commemorated on this day are among those about whom little is known, except for their mention in the gospels. James the Less is so called to distinguish him from James the son of Zebedee and from James "the brother of the Lord," or perhaps to indicate youth or lack of stature. He is known to us from the list of the Twelve, where he is called James the son of Alpheus. He may also be the person referred to in Mark's Gospel as James the younger, who, with his mother Mary and the other women, watched the crucifixion from a distance.

Philip figures in several important incidents in Jesus' ministry as reported in John's Gospel. There we read that Jesus called Philip soon after calling Andrew and Peter. Philip, in turn, found his friend Nathanael, and convinced him to come and see Jesus, the Messiah. Later, when Jesus saw the hungry crowd, he asked Philip, "Where are we to buy bread for these people to eat?" (John 6:5). Philip's practical response, "Six months' wages would not buy enough bread for each of them to get a little" (John 6:7), was the prelude to the feeding of the multitude with the loaves and fishes. In a later incident in John's Gospel, some Greeks came to Philip asking to see Jesus. At the Last Supper, Philip's request, "Lord, show us the Father, and we will be satisfied," evokes the response, "Have I been with you all this time, Philip, and you still do not know me? Whoever has seen me has seen the Father" (John 14:8,9).

Pray

Almighty God, who gave to your apostles Philip and James grace and strength to bear witness to the truth: Grant that we, being mindful of their victory of faith, may glorify in life and death the Name of our Lord Jesus Christ; who lives and reigns with you and the Holy Spirit, one God, now and for ever. *Amen.*

Ascension Day

*This date changes each year.
Check your calendar to determine the date.*

Read

Psalm 47 *or* 93 | Acts 1:1-11
Ephesians 1:15-23 | Luke 24:44-53

Reflect

Today we celebrate the Ascension, the day Jesus is lifted up in a cloud from the earth and taken into heaven in the sight of his disciples. Just before Jesus takes flight, the disciples have their chance to catch up on the last of Jesus' personally offered teachings and have been promised the Holy Spirit. They have been blessed by Jesus, and then he ascends into heaven.

Author

Lauren Kuratko is an Episcopal priest in New York who enjoys outdoor adventures with her husband and three exuberant boys, every single second of quiet she can find, and cheering for Auburn football.

In the retelling of this story in Acts chapter one, after Jesus ascends, the disciples are staring up toward the heavens when two men in white robes appear. They ask the disciples:

"Why do you stand looking up toward heaven?"

I love this line of scripture! "Why do you stand looking up toward heaven?" It feels like the disciples are getting called out in school, reminded to stop daydreaming and start paying attention to the lesson. Yes, Jesus has ascended, and I can only imagine it looked pretty amazing. And now he's out of sight, and they are just staring at the sky. *Why are you staring at the sky when there are things to do here right before your eyes?*

Sometimes, in parenting and working with children, I need to have this same reminder.

Why are you staring at the sky?

Why are you so looking forward to the end of the school year and summer plans (I still can't believe our school does not finish until the end of June!)?

Or, why are you looking forward to the time when the kids are a bit older?

Wonderful children of God stand before us right now, needing our attention in this moment and not our glassy-eyed stare at the heavens.

Have you had this experience? Perhaps when your children were babies and would not sleep through the night. "I can't wait until they get older," we think, "so we all can get a good night's sleep." Or perhaps when toddlers are being terrible twos or three-nagers, we think, "Gosh, won't things be better when they go to elementary school, and they can better express their emotions?"

There is always a next milestone to look toward. We can spend most of our lives looking toward the heavens, waiting for the next threshold to be crossed. However, when we do that, we miss being in the present moment. There are times in our present moment that can be tiring, hilarious, or soul-wearying. And yet, they usually offer a glimmer of goodness in our present moment, too.

Our present moment isn't only diapers, three-nager tantrums, and uncool parents. It's also that baby-smell, the insightful observations of toddlers, and the growing independence of grade school. Like the disciples, sometimes we need to be reminded to look around us *right now.* We, like the disciples, have listened to Jesus' teachings, been promised the Holy Spirit, been blessed by God, and been given our mission in the world. Our task is not to stare into heaven but to look around us right now, guiding the children in our lives and letting them guide us.

Respond

Consider celebrating Ascension Day with a cloud cake (any cake with a lot of white, fluffy frosting) topped with a hand-drawn Jesus. Bake the cake together (or buy one!), then sit outside and read the story of the Ascension from Acts. As you're reading, lift the cake to the heavens. You might read a favorite poem or two or sing an Ascension Day hymn, and then share some cake. Here are some suggested readings: Acts 1:1-11, Jesus Ascends into Heaven; Psalm 47 on God, King of the World; Psalm 93 on the Splendor of God; Luke 24:44-53, the

Ascension of Jesus; The Collect for Ascension Day in *The Book of Common Prayer;* A "Sonnet for Ascension Day" by Malcolm Guite; "Ascension Day" by Christina Georgina Rossetti; and "Ascension" by John Donne

Learn More

Ascension Day occurs on a Thursday each year forty days after Easter Day, marking the conclusion of Jesus' earthly life and his ascension into heaven. It is one of the seven principal feasts in the Episcopal Church. We read about Jesus' ascension in the gospels of Luke and Mark and the Acts of the Apostles. Both the Nicene and Apostles' creeds include the ascension of Jesus into heaven, as he concludes his post-resurrection appearances and ascends into the nearer presence of God. Saint Augustine of Hippo preaches about Ascension Day in the early fifth century in a way that implies it was universally observed by Christians long before his lifetime.

Pray

Almighty God, whose blessed Son our Savior Jesus Christ ascended far above all heavens that he might fill all things: Mercifully give us faith to perceive that, according to his promise, he abides with his Church on earth, even to the end of the ages; through Jesus Christ our Lord, who lives and reigns with you and the Holy Spirit, one God, in glory everlasting. *Amen.*

—The Book of Common Prayer

DAY OF PENTECOST

This date changes each year.
Check your calendar to determine the date.

Read

Psalm 104:25-35, 37 | Acts 2:1-21 *or* Numbers 11:24-30
1 Corinthians 12:3b-13 *or* Acts 2:1-21
John 20:19-23 *or* 7:37-39 (Year A)

Psalm 104:25-35, 37 | Acts 2:1-21 *or* Ezekiel 37:1-14
Romans 8:22-27 *or* Acts 2:1-21
John 15:26-27; 16:4b-15 (Year B)

Psalm 104:25-35, 37 | Acts 2:1-21 *or* Genesis 11:1-9
Romans 8:14-17 *or* Acts 2:1-21
John 14:8-17, (25-27) (Year C)

Author

Sara Irwin, an Episcopal priest, is mother to Isaiah and Adah, and spouse to Noah Evans; they live near Pittsburgh, Pennsylvania. She loves tattoos, hiking, and making beer.

Reflect

My daughter has a book about unusual animal friendships. It hits every mark for cuteness: miniature animals, golden retrievers, unlikely successes. Rather than being sticky-sweet, though, the book offers a generosity of spirit. Animals are delightful, but wherever you find it, the redemptive nature of love is no joke.

The other day we read a story about a mean, biting miniature horse (Spanky) who finds friendship and reconciliation with an obnoxious terrier puppy (Dally). One day the dog launches itself up onto the miniature horse's back (it's not quite three feet tall), and from then on, they are inseparable. Where the humans and other horses have failed to domesticate the horse, the dog succeeds. While humans have failed to manage the dog's constant barking and anxiety, the horse teaches him a sense of calm and discipline. There's a real sense of hope; the stories are so implausible that you can't help but think everything will be okay. Reading the book with my children this week, it struck me that these animals are a Pentecost story; somehow, they speak each other's language.

When the early church gathers, they know something is brewing, that Jesus will make a new thing happen as they reassemble themselves after the Ascension. But they cannot possibly imagine the tongues of fire, and they definitely are not planning on that multilingual riot of sound.

Pentecost offers a truth we so often resist: the dream of God is of diversity, not sameness.

The different languages spoken by the people of Jerusalem are intact; the crowd does not suddenly break into Greek or Aramaic so they can communicate together. The gift is the *bridging* of difference, not its erasure. Pentecost tells us, once and for all, that we don't have to be the same.

In our human limitation, we long for conformity and fear difference. But the Pentecost story is the Spirit giving us the gift of ourselves, *as* ourselves, alongside others. This is a hard lesson to absorb as an adult and a place where we are often led by our children. How often do we look for refuge in sameness rather than listening for what comes between us? How often do we mute aspects of ourselves for fear of judgment, when our kids openly disagree, argue, and reconcile?

This is not to silence the truth of sin. For those who suffer oppression because of race or gender identity or religion or sexuality, being who they are openly can be literally life-threatening Pentecost gives not only a gift, but a charge, to build a world where the Spirit can move. Pentecost calls us to open our ears as well as our hearts, to move our feet as well as our mouths.

This Pentecost, of course, I want to receive the Holy Spirit. I'll wear red shoes under my alb (I'm an all-black kind of person, so this will be a stretch). I'll pray for the birthday of the church and implausible prophecy and love across difference. And if a miniature horse comes and bites me, I will know to look for a puppy to calm it down.

Respond

Doves are a common symbol of Pentecost. One way to celebrate the feast day is to make a banner of doves. Take a large piece of watercolor paper, tape it firmly to a board or table, wet the whole paper, and then drop dollops of watercolor paint onto the sheet. The result, once dry, is a bright and beautiful rainbow of colors.

Cut several doves out of the paper, and on each dove, write the words love, peace, and hope in different languages. This is a reminder that the Holy Spirit came down and gave the apostles the ability to spread the Good News in languages from around the world.

Hole punch each dove and pull a piece of thread through the doves and then hang your banner as a symbol of God's love that reaches out to all.

Learn More

The Day of Pentecost, which falls fifty days after Easter, is the remembrance of the coming of the Holy Spirit among the apostles, described in Acts 2. On the Day of Pentecost, Christians celebrate the Holy Spirit, which inspired and empowered the followers of Jesus to do the work of Christ in the world.

The Holy Spirit is the "giver of life" in that the Spirit was present from the moment of creation and continues to be one of the ways God animates us with God's presence. The Nicene Creed says that the Spirit is worthy of worship and praise and emphasizes how the prophets through time have been the Holy Spirit's voice.

The Day of Pentecost kicks off a long season sometimes referred to as Ordinary Time, not because it is mundane but because the church counts the Sundays using "ordinal numbers"— Second Sunday after Pentecost, Third Sunday after Pentecost, etc. This is a season for growth, a reminder that the long walk of faith isn't always highs and lows but is made up of the stuff of everyday life. The Last Sunday after Pentecost marks the end of the church year, then the church heads into Advent to begin the cycle again.

—*Walk in Love: Episcopal Beliefs & Practices*,
published by Forward Movement

Pray

Almighty God, on this day you opened the way of eternal life to every race and nation by the promised gift of your Holy Spirit: Shed abroad this gift throughout the world by the preaching of the Gospel, that it may reach to the ends of the earth; through Jesus Christ our Lord, who lives and reigns with you, in the unity of the Holy Spirit, one God, for ever and ever. *Amen.*

—*The Book of Common Prayer*

The Visitation of the Blessed Virgin Mary

Read

Psalm 113 | 1 Samuel 2:1-10
Romans 12:9-16b | Luke 1:39-57

Reflect

There were exactly two snowballs in my south Louisiana childhood, and they didn't fall from the sky in Baton Rouge.

They rode down from Ohio on the side of our neighbor's station wagon and took their shape when she scooped them and gave them to wide-eyed children who had never seen snow.

It must have been right before bath time, because that's where I remember looking with envy at the snowball in my sister's hands—still white and big and magical. Mine was gray now, icy and smaller, because I had dipped it in the water. I was *this* close to talking her into switching; I really think I was convincing her she would like the gray one better, when my mother intervened.

Author
Ann Benton Fraser, an Episcopal priest, lives with her husband Andrew and their three children in San Antonio, Texas. She spends time reading, being outside, and learning from her children.

Dang it. I couldn't even see her magical treasure anymore, because I was stuck with this other one I had ruined.

Today is the Feast of the Visitation, that encounter between Elizabeth and her cousin Mary that we read about in the first chapter of Luke. We are told in that story that Mary went to visit her relative:

> When Elizabeth heard Mary's greeting, the child leaped in her womb. And Elizabeth was filled with the Holy Spirit and exclaimed with a loud cry, "Blessed are you among women, and blessed is the fruit of your womb. And why has this happened to me, that the mother of my Lord comes to me? For as soon as I heard the sound of your greeting, the child in my womb leaped for joy. And blessed is she who believed that there would be a fulfillment of what was spoken to her by the Lord" (Luke 1:41-46).

Elizabeth has an inner reaction of joy in response to Mary, a surging of Spirit-goodness that blesses both of them. It feels like a charming and loving story to me—this unscripted happiness, the knowing between the older kinswoman and her younger relative.

Surely Elizabeth had anticipation and joy of her own, at the long-awaited child in her womb. The angel who proclaimed this child's coming had said he would be great in the eyes of God and that he would turn hearts in love and wisdom toward the Lord. This child would be important not only to her but to the faith of many.

Surely she had burdens to share like how her husband Zechariah had been struck silent when he could not believe the angel's promise. She prepared for this child's arrival without the comfort of her partner's conversation, in the loneliness of that quiet.

And yet, there is room for the Spirit to move through all these things. At the mere sound of Mary's voice, Elizabeth recognizes and blesses her for bearing witness to God's faithfulness.

Religious art depicts many beautiful images of these women together, often clinging lovingly to one another, arms clasped. My favorites are the delightful icons that show the mothers embracing while babies in utero regard one another with a bow or a leap and a blessing in return.

When gratitude swells within us, it's a wonderful thing. Isn't that the gracious Spirit of God making itself known within us, in response to the world around us? But sometimes we are stuck, missing that Spirit-movement because all we can see is the thing we don't have.

Anybody who spends time with children knows what dedicated accountants they can be, especially when it comes to measuring a sibling's advantage.

As I ponder the visitation story, I wonder how we can practice in our families being free to be happy for someone else. Not long ago, one of my children got something the other did not. The one without definitely noticed. It wasn't fair.

Should we get a second Something?

It was reasonable: this was a thing we could afford, we could find easily, and we knew would be used. Hey, here's a situation I can fix!

But when the child who did not get the Something shared her sadness and frustration with me, the Holy Spirit grabbed the snowplow keys out of my hand. You know that parenting instinct to plow obstacles out of the way for our children, so their path is smooth and safe?

I hugged her close to me when I said, "Sometimes it's someone else's turn to have something special, and that can be hard."

The opportunity to navigate disappointment may be a more enduring gift than the object of our desire could be. We don't always leap with joy at another's good fortune, especially when we long for that same fortune for ourselves.

We didn't get all the way to happy-for-you in our conversation about the Something. But maybe there was something small within, the tiniest bow, the littlest of leaps.

Respond

Plan a visit with longtime friends, perhaps some you haven't seen in a while. You might pack a picnic lunch or pick some flowers to add extra delight to the visit. While you're together, take some time to reminisce about your friendship, how it began, and how it has blessed you.

Learn More

This feast commemorates the visit of the Blessed Virgin to her cousin Elizabeth, recorded in the Gospel according to Luke (1:39-56).

Elizabeth, who was then pregnant with John the Baptist, greeted Mary with the words, "Blessed are you among women, and blessed is the fruit of your womb." Mary broke into the song of praise and thanksgiving which we call the *Magnificat*, "My soul proclaims the greatness of the Lord."

In this scene, the unborn John the Baptist, the prophet who was to prepare the way of the Lord, rejoices in the presence of him whose coming he is later to herald publicly to all Israel, for the gospel records that when Mary's greeting came to her kinswoman's ears, the babe in Elizabeth's womb leaped for joy.

Pray

Father in heaven, by your grace the virgin mother of your incarnate Son was blessed in bearing him, but still more blessed in keeping your word: Grant us who honor the exaltation of her lowliness to follow the example of her devotion to your will; through Jesus Christ our Lord, who lives and reigns with you and the Holy Spirit, one God, for ever and ever. *Amen.*

TRINITY SUNDAY

This date changes each year.
Check your calendar to determine the date.

Read

Psalm 8 | Genesis 1:1—2:4a *or* Canticle 2 *or* 13
2 Corinthians 13:11-13
Matthew 28:16-20 (Year A)

Psalm 29 | Isaiah 6:1-8 *or* Canticle 2 *or* 13
Romans 8:12-17 | John 3:1-17 (Year B)

Psalm 8 | Proverbs 8:1-4, 22-31 *or* Canticle 2 *or* 13
Romans 5:1-5 | John 16:12-15 (Year C)

Author

Christina (Tina) Clark lives in Denver, Colorado, has two teenage sons, and loves all things church, the Rocky Mountains, and the Pacific Ocean.

Reflect

"Tina, how many gods do we worship?"

I was recently asked this question, in utter sincerity, by a thirteen-year-old in my youth group.

This young lady has been an Episcopalian since toddlerhood. She's grown up right here in our church, attending Sunday School and youth group. She serves as an acolyte.

Dismayed, my initial reaction was less than graceful. "One!" I blurted. Then I took a breath and followed with, "Why do you ask?"

"My friend said we worship three gods, because we say 'Father, Son, and Holy Spirit.'"

Aha.

Uh oh.

How do I explain the Trinity to a bright-but-still-concrete young teen? Without committing heresy? I know clergy who take vacation days to avoid preaching on Trinity Sunday. I've watched ordained adults play "rock, paper, scissors," with the loser giving the homily on Trinity Sunday. If they're so reluctant to tackle the sacred mystery of the Holy Three-in-One, who was I to take it on unprepared?

I've approached the Trinity with children before, tentatively. Once a lovely grandmother showed me how to cut a mobius strip just right to create three interconnected rings: three rings, all attached but perceptible, from one piece of paper. I repeated that craft perfectly, once, while practicing alone, and never got it right again. I kept ending up with two interconnected rings, the third falling away, severed from the original paper. I never used it with kids.

Many Christians like the clover analogy often attributed to Saint Patrick. A clover is one plant; its three distinct leaves can represent the Father, Son, and Holy Spirit being separate yet all a part of something larger than itself. Unfortunately, it's actually "partialism," one of several Trinitarian heresies, because it makes each of the persons of the Trinity only part God, able to become fully God only when they're all together.

Standing there with this youth who needed an answer from me, I remembered my favorite thing about my life as a teacher, a parent, and a family minister: I don't have to know all the answers!

Finally, shooting off a quick prayer for guidance and forgiveness, I told my young friend what I understand—and what I don't.

I think the Trinity is all about God's infinite ability to meet us—each of us, all the time—exactly where we are, with divine understanding that we aren't always in the same place. Our emotional needs change, not just from childhood to adulthood but in a constant ebb and flow as life challenges and upholds us. God made us, and by God, we are well-loved. God's perfect knowledge and care of us includes knowing that we require more than a single image or manifestation of God's divine presence.

Sometimes, I need God, the Father. I need that ideal parent who loves me no matter what, who believes in my ability to be who God asks me to be, and who stands with and behind me as I walk the journey of this life. Like a good parent, God lets me make mistakes and is there for me when I regret and learn and move on from them. Young children tend to believe their parents are all-knowing and all-powerful, and they feel a sense of safety in that belief. As adults, we know differently— yet our parents are often still the people we call when we need sympathy, unconditional support, and encouragement. Part of our humanity is a deep need to be lovingly parented.

Other times, I need God, the Redeemer. The Christ who was born and grew and lived a fully human life, even in his divinity, and died in pain and sorrow and suffering. Who got angry when people failed to understand how to love God and love each other. Who needed the soothing comfort of that expensive oil before going to his brutal condemnation and death. I need Christ's humanity to remind me that my own is sacred.

Often, for me, the ethereal divinity of the Holy Spirit is the most visceral impression of God's presence. I can feel the Holy Spirit around us when we raise our voices together in prayer and hymn. In meditative prayer, I feel and see soothing light: God coming to me as Holy Spirit. In meetings, I pray for the Holy Spirit to come amongst the group gathered and inspire us to be the people God calls us to be and do the work God calls us to do.

So there's my answer, such as it is. There is one God. That God created us and knows us, and thus comes to us as a Trinity, allowing us to meet God—Father, Son, and Holy Spirit—wherever we are in the moment.

Respond

Look up the various symbols for the Trinity. Draw your favorite ones or make a collage of all of them!

Learn More

Trinity Sunday, the Sunday following the Day of Pentecost, celebrates the gift of God's threefold nature: Father, Son, and Holy Spirit. Holy Trinity is a divine mystery. At its core, the Holy Trinity reveals that God is a God of relationship. Father, Son, and Holy Spirit are in a beautiful, careful, and timeless dance. The Holy Trinity reveals that God is unity, diversity, and majesty.

Trinity Sunday is now one of the seven principal feasts of the church year, but it took a thousand years for Christians to embrace this holy mystery. Earliest records of its observance date to the tenth century, but it gained popularity in the West after Pope John XXII added it to the Roman Catholic Church calendar in 1334.

—*Walk in Love: Episcopal Beliefs & Practices*,
published by Forward Movement

Pray

Almighty and everlasting God, you have given to us your servants grace, by the confession of a true faith, to acknowledge the glory of the eternal Trinity, and in the power of your divine Majesty to worship the Unity: Keep us steadfast in this faith and worship, and bring us at last to see you in your one and eternal glory, O Father; who with the Son and the Holy Spirit live and reign, one God, for ever and ever. *Amen.*

—*The Book of Common Prayer*

Saint Barnabas the Apostle

Read

Psalm 112 | Isaiah 42:5-12
Acts 11:19-30; 13:1-3 | Matthew 10:7-16

Reflect

Saint Barnabas, one of the earliest apostles, is mostly a supporting actor in the story of the early church. In the drama of those first years following Pentecost, he receives fewer lines of dialogue than our main characters, Peter or Paul. Plus, his character is not as heroically depicted for any grand act of miracle or sacrifice, such as the striking down of Ananias or the martyrdom of Stephen. Yet his presence is noted in a lot of scenes in the early Christian story, especially in the Acts of the Apostles. Even as a supporting cast member, Barnabas's role is irreplaceable in the development and spread of Christianity.

Author
Ben Day, an Episcopal priest, is an avid reader, cyclist, and runner and single father to a young son, Marshall. They live in Kennesaw, Georgia.

Take for example Saul's return to Jerusalem after the Damascus road experience: it is Barnabas who vouches for the sincerity of his conversion and helps convince the other apostles to accept him (Acts 9:27). Where would Christianity be without Saint Paul the Apostle and his writings and witness? Barnabas's support gets him started and legitimizes him as an insider and apostle.

Or consider the missionary journeys to Antioch and beyond, recorded later in the Acts of the Apostles (chapters 13 and 14). Barnabas and Paul set out together to spread the message of Jesus. It is Paul who converts the governor of Cyprus by striking the sorcerer, Bar-Jesus, blind. And it is again Paul who makes the stirring speech in the synagogue of Pisidia, but Barnabas is at his side through the whole journey.

Barnabas is not just Paul's stagnant sidekick, though, because he is cited as part of the exhortation in every place they stop. Throughout the whole journey, in fact, Barnabas gets no dialogue or billing of just his own, yet he stands with Paul and is consistently attributed to the exhortations in each place the Spirit led them, and his name is cited seventeen times in those eighty verses. Barnabas is not merely an extra or "also-ran" in Christianity's spread. He is a minor character with a big influence.

In noticing this dynamic in the recorded life and ministry of Barnabas, my family has adopted a gratitude practice of "seeing" in our minds those who sometimes go unseen. We share the names of these supporters with each other as we prepare dinner or get ready for bed in the evenings. Who in our work, our home, or our play is standing with us to empower our work and encourage our calls but is maybe not being noticed?

As a parish rector, many stand with me as witness and supporter. A dozen or more parishioners are at everything we do in my parish. They come if the doors are open. Many of them are not in formal leadership positions, but they still stand with me in the ministry and operations of witnessing in my faith community and beyond.

For example, there is the lady who makes sure fresh flowers are growing on my walk to and from the rectory. This ministry of presence has often lifted my spirits. Two gentlemen sort our cans and recycling and take it to the scrap yard for reuse. They serve us—and save us time and expense.

My ex-wife is an attorney who works with a mostly indigent population of offenders with severe and persistent mental health challenges. The secretary at the courthouse always greets her with a story or kind word; she is someone who stands with her. There is also the consultant who checks in every month or so, even though his work finished a couple of years ago and he isn't on the payroll anymore. Plus, there's the mom of an offender who died who took the time to write what the court's kindness and compassion to her son meant to their whole family. That letter stays with her team as an inspiration to continue their work of kindness and compassion. Those are people who "stand with" her in her call.

In the afternoons, when I pick up our three-year-old son from daycare, I ask who he played with today and wait patiently as he sorts through his day with teachers and peers. This is a practice we hope will instill in him a mindful appreciation of those who stand with him in fun and play.

All of these people named, from the gardener to my sons' teachers and peers, are people who are supporting actors in the drama of our lives. Without them, we would not be able to be who God called us to be in the same way. Their gifts and ministry are irreplaceable, as much as Barnabas was to the start of the church.

Respond

On this feast day of Saint Barnabas, take a moment to reflect on the supporting actors of your life and work. Who stands with you, but without much notice? Who makes your Christian life and call possible?

Draw or write a thank you note to those people today. Make sure to drop the letters in the mail or hand deliver. The next time you gather with your family and pray, make sure to list these supporters by name. By sharing our supporters, might we all grow in awareness of the Barnabases of our day.

Learn More

"There was a Levite, a native of Cyprus, Joseph, to whom the apostles gave the name Barnabas (which means "son of encouragement"). He sold a field that belonged to him, then brought the money, and laid it at the apostles' feet" (Acts 4:36-37). This first reference in the New Testament to Barnabas introduces one whose missionary efforts would cause him to be called, like the Twelve, an apostle.

As a Jew of the diaspora, Barnabas had much in common with Paul. When Paul came to Jerusalem after his conversion, the disciples were afraid to receive him. It was Barnabas who brought Paul to the apostles, and declared to them how, on the road to Damascus, Paul had seen the Lord, and had preached boldly in the name of Jesus (Acts 9:27). Later, Barnabas, having settled in Antioch, sent for Paul to join him in leading the Christian church in that city.

Barnabas and Paul were sent by the disciples in Antioch to carry famine relief to the church in Jerusalem. Upon their return, the church in Antioch sent them on their first missionary journey beginning at Cyprus. At Lystra in Asia Minor, the people took them to be gods, supposing the eloquent Paul to be Mercury, the messenger of the gods, and Barnabas to be Jupiter, the chief of the gods, a testimony to the commanding presence of Barnabas.

The association of Barnabas and Paul was broken, after their journey, by a disagreement about Mark, who had left the mission to return to Jerusalem. After attending the Council of Jerusalem with Barnabas, Paul made a return visit to the churches that he and Barnabas had founded in Asia Minor. Barnabas and Mark went to Cyprus, where Barnabas is traditionally honored as the founder of the church. Tradition has it that he was martyred at Salamis in Cyprus.

Pray

Grant, O God, that we may follow the example of your faithful servant Barnabas, who, seeking not his own renown but the well-being of your church, gave generously of his life and substance for the relief of the poor and the spread of the Gospel; through Jesus Christ our Lord, who lives and reigns with you and the Holy Spirit, one God, for ever and ever. *Amen.*

The Nativity of Saint John the Baptist

Read

Psalm 85 *or* 85:7-13 | Isaiah 40:1-11
Acts 13:14b-26 | Luke 1:57-80

Reflect

Today the church celebrates the feast of the Nativity of Saint John the Baptist, Christ's forerunner. Saint John the Baptist is unlike many saints on our calendar because we celebrate his ministry on the day of his birth rather than the day of his death. His birth is worth celebrating. The entire first chapter of the Gospel according to Luke is primarily the story that leads to this feast day:

- Elizabeth and Zechariah, though blameless before God, have no children;

- Zechariah is visited by an angel of the Lord who foretells the birth of a child to be named John;

Author

Nurya Love Parish is an Episcopal priest and ministry developer and was the founding editor of Grow Christians. She has reached the late teenage stage of parenting with her firefighter husband, and they live in Rockford, Michigan.

- Zechariah questions the prophecy and is struck dumb;

- Elizabeth does conceive, six months before Mary herself is given a child by the Holy Spirit;

- Mary visits Elizabeth and offers her song of praise to God (later called the *Magnificat*);

- Elizabeth gives birth and declares the child will be named John;

- Zechariah agrees, writing John's name and regaining his ability to speak;

- Zechariah offers his song of praise to God (later called the *Benedictus Dominus Deus*);

- And the infant John arrives in the world, ready to turn it upside down (as Presiding Bishop Michael Curry would say: which is right side up again).

We know what comes next: John's own preaching, the ministry of baptism he offers for repentance and forgiveness of sins, his baptizing Jesus in the River Jordan, his challenging teachings, his imprisonment by Herod, and his beheading. We know and honor his whole story today.

This feast day means, among other things, that Christmas is six months away, because John was six months older than Jesus: the one who fully and finally turned the world right side up again.

Growing Christians

What strikes me is both how ordinary and how extraordinary this scene is. Attended by women, recently delivered of her first and only child, Elizabeth looks on as her husband writes his name. The scripture says that she had already decided to name her son John; now, her husband is about to agree. Just as we fill out birth certificates, he has formed the second letter of John's name.

Why did naming this child John matter? The name John is our modern English version of the name that Elizabeth and Zechariah would have used, Johanan. The name means "God is gracious." If there is one thing John the Baptist preached and practiced, it was the grace of God. We remember him not only for his deeds but also his words, among them: "Whoever has two coats must share with anyone who has none; and whoever has food must do likewise" (Luke 3:11).

Because God in grace has provided for us, we are generous to provide for others. There is always a very practical aspect to repentance and salvation. Saint John the Baptist knew that—and so do we.

Respond

Wonder aloud what Zechariah and Elizabeth felt upon learning of the pregnancy and what plans they dreamed for their long-awaited miracle child. Share your memories from the time you learned your children were coming into your life, how you chose their names, and the dreams you created for them.

Learn More

John the Baptist, the prophet, and forerunner of Jesus, was the son of elderly parents, Elizabeth and Zechariah, and according to the Gospel of Luke, he was related to Jesus on his mother's side. His birth is celebrated six months before Christmas Day, since, according to Luke, Elizabeth became pregnant six months before the angel Gabriel appeared to Mary. John figures prominently in all four gospels, but the account of his birth is given only in the Gospel according to Luke. His father, Zechariah, a priest of the Temple at Jerusalem, was struck speechless because he doubted a vision foretelling John's birth. When his speech was restored, Zechariah uttered a canticle of praise, the Benedictus, which is one of the canticles used in the Daily Office, traditionally at Morning Prayer.

John lived ascetically in the desert. He was clothed with camel's hair, with a leather belt, and ate locusts and wild honey. He preached repentance, and called upon people to prepare for the coming of the Kingdom and of the Messiah, baptizing his followers to signify their repentance and new life. Jesus himself was baptized by John in the Jordan River.

John is remembered during Advent as a prophet, and at Epiphany as the baptizer of Jesus. The Gospel according to John quotes the Baptist as saying to his followers that Jesus is the Lamb of God, and prophesying, "He must increase, but I must decrease" (John 3:30).

Growing Christians

Pray

Almighty God, by whose providence your servant John the Baptist was wonderfully born, and sent to prepare the way of your Son our Savior by preaching repentance: Make us so to follow his teaching and holy life, that we may truly repent according to his preaching; and, following his example, constantly speak the truth, boldly rebuke vice, and patiently suffer for the truth's sake; through Jesus Christ your Son our Lord, who lives and reigns with you and the Holy Spirit, one God, for ever and ever. *Amen.*

JUNE 29

Saint Peter and Saint Paul, Apostles

Read

Psalm 87 | Ezekiel 34:11-16
2 Timothy 4:1-8 | John 21:15-19

Reflect

"Kale yeah!" I couldn't help but shout joyfully! The kiddos rolled their eyes and shook their heads at me.

Author

Dorian Del Priore is an Episcopal priest who has been involved in youth ministry for more than twenty years. Dorian is a husband to Lauren and a father to Jordan and Brynn, and they live in Columbia, South Carolina.

Hundreds of pounds of kale at the food bank needed to be sorted into appropriate portions to hand out to clients. Food banks often need volunteers to sort enormous pallets of kale, apples, and other produce donated from local farmers. I find that sorting donations at a food bank is a lot of fun: music, dancing, jokes, and laughter make for joyful work. It also feels right and good, putting flesh and bones on the words we pray and the lessons we learn inside the walls of the church.

Growing Christians

The Feast of Saint Peter and Saint Paul celebrates two evangelistic icons of the early church. The origins of this shared feast day point to their common martyrdom in Rome, Peter in 64 CE by inverted crucifixion and Paul in 67 CE by beheading.

Peter and Paul also have a commonality in the beginnings of the journeys following Jesus. When Jesus calls Peter, he says, "Come, follow me." To Saul (soon to be Paul) on the road to Damascus, the risen Jesus says, "Now get up and go." Following Jesus has a kinetic nature to it for each.

Discipleship in the way of Jesus is kinesthetic. It requires movement. Discipleship engages the body; learning is tactile and engaging. Life in the way of Jesus is an embodied faith.

When Jesus called Peter to follow, Peter steps into a way of life that is lived on the road, in the world, and amongst people. With Jesus, Peter and the disciples feed the hungry, heal the sick, reach out to the lost, and love the broken. The journey takes them to villages, mountains, the countryside, on boats, and into remarkable situations.

When Jesus calls Paul, Paul embarks on a journey of preaching and engagement with communities. Paul's missionary travels take him far and wide. Paul wants to share his experience of the risen Jesus with as many people as possible. His feet take his message from Arabia to Spain.

Like Peter and Paul, our life in the way of Jesus is lived out through our bodies. From worship to service, we have ample opportunities to walk beside and with our children and be formed together by the movements and sensations associated with our tradition.

Our liturgy is kinetic and tactile, engaging the fullness of our senses. We kneel, bow, and make the sign of the cross. Prayers soak our hearts, and hymns ring in our ears. We watch the prayers of incense rise as the smell of holiness fills our spirits. We see bread blessed and broken, we drink from the cup of salvation, and we eat the bread of heaven. What we do in worship and how we pray shapes our beliefs and how we live out our lives in faith.

Faith lived out through service requires movement outside sanctuaries also. From preparing meals in soup kitchens to washing clothes in a laundromat, from painting and hammering at construction projects to sorting donations at food banks, we engage in discipleship that is kinetic and tactile by nature. When we serve as families and communities, we model how love for another intimately dovetails with our love for God.

A kinetic, embodied faith follows in the footsteps of Jesus. Paul, in Romans, more than hints at this when he quotes Isaiah and writes: "How beautiful are the feet of those who bring good news!"

Worshiping together and serving alongside my kids at food banks, soup kitchens, laundromats, and construction sites has helped us to develop a deeper sense of God's calling in our lives and what it means to live life in the way of Jesus. The kinesthetic nature of an embodied faith drives home in

Growing Christians

particular ways that we fulfill the law of Christ when we help carry the burdens of others.

Martyrdom is a difficult, and probably scary, topic to explain to children. However, on this Feast of Saint Peter and Saint Paul, we can also explain sacrifice with a different approach. Sacrificial love is an embodied faith lived for the benefit of other people. As disciples and parents, we have the incredible opportunity to practice living it out together with the next generation of disciples, side by side. Tired feet and dirty hands make for a joyful heart and a soul that overflows with God's love and grace.

Can I get a kale yeah?!

Respond

Research the topic of food deserts. If you live in or near one, talk about the challenges of it. If you have plenty of options for good and healthy food, explore with each other what it might be like if those resources were gone. Then, talk about how you might contribute to a solution. This might include volunteering at a local food bank (even sorting the kale!) or serving in a soup kitchen.

Learn More

Peter and Paul, the two greatest leaders of the early church, are also commemorated separately, Peter on January 18, for his confession of Jesus as the Messiah, and Paul on January 25, for his conversion, but they are commemorated together on June 29 in observance of the tradition of the church that they both died as martyrs in Rome during the persecution under Nero in 64 CE.

Paul, the well-educated and cosmopolitan Jew of the diaspora, and Peter, the uneducated fisherman from Galilee, had differences of opinion in the early years of the church concerning the mission to the Gentiles. More than once, Paul speaks of rebuking Peter for his continued insistence on Jewish exclusiveness; yet their common commitment to Christ and the proclamation of the gospel proved stronger than their differences; and both eventually carried that mission to Rome, where they were martyred. According to tradition, Paul was granted the right of a Roman citizen to be beheaded by a sword, but Peter suffered the fate of his Lord, crucifixion, although with his head downward.

A generation after their martyrdom, Clement of Rome, writing to the church in Corinth, probably in the year 96, wrote: "Let us come to those who have most recently proved champions; let us take up the noble examples of our own generation. Because of jealousy and envy the greatest and most upright pillars of the church were persecuted and competed unto death. Let us bring before our eyes the good apostles—Peter, who because of unrighteous jealousy endured not one or two, but numerous trials, and so bore a martyr's witness and went to the glorious place that he deserved. Because of jealousy and strife Paul pointed the way to the reward of endurance; seven times he was imprisoned, he was exiled, he was stoned, he was a preacher in both East and West, and won renown for his faith, teaching uprightness to the whole world, and reaching the farthest limit of the West, and bearing a martyr's witness before the rulers, he passed out of the world and was taken up into the holy place, having proved a very great example of endurance."

Pray

Almighty God, whose blessed apostles Peter and Paul glorified you by their martyrdom: Grant that your Church, instructed by their teaching and example, and knit together in unity by your Spirit, may ever stand firm upon the one foundation, which is Jesus Christ our Lord; who lives and reigns with you, in the unity of the same Spirit, one God, now and for ever. *Amen.*

July 4

Independence Day (USA)

Read

Psalm 145 *or* 145:1-9 | Deuteronomy 10:17-21
Hebrews 11:8-16 | Matthew 5:43-48

Reflect

Independence Day is a major feast according to the calendar of the Episcopal Church. Until I started editing the *Grow Christians* blog, I was unaware of this reality. When I discovered it, I found it slightly disturbing. And then I thought again.

I was born in 1971. And so I come to participation in American civic life with the recognition that American civic life is deeply flawed—and always has been.

I am not part of that generation that was taught to honor God and country in the same breath. I am part of a generation that studied the civil rights movement starting in

> **Author**
>
> **Nurya Love Parish** is an Episcopal priest and ministry developer and was the founding editor of Grow Christians. She has reached the late teenage stage of parenting with her firefighter husband, and they live in Rockford, Michigan.

elementary school. Early on I learned the words of the Rev. Dr. Martin Luther King Jr.:

> When the architects of our republic wrote the magnificent words of the Constitution and the Declaration of Independence, they were signing a promissory note to which every American was to fall heir. This note was a promise that all men, yes, Black men as well as white men, would be guaranteed the inalienable rights of life, liberty, and the pursuit of happiness.

It is obvious today that America has defaulted on this promissory note insofar as her citizens of color are concerned.

When you learn as a child that your country has been broken from the beginning—not only from speeches but from incontrovertible facts, not only in regard to the rights of Black men but also many more—you come to Independence Day with a certain wariness.

And yet.

And yet our church teaches us to honor this day. That means we approach it in faith as disciples of Jesus Christ. The gospel lesson appointed for today contains some of the most challenging words he spoke:

> "You have heard that it was said, 'You shall love your neighbor and hate your enemy.' But I say to you, Love your enemies and pray for those who persecute you, so that you may be children of your Father in heaven; for he makes his sun rise on the evil and on the good,

and sends rain on the righteous and on the unrighteous. For if you love those who love you, what reward do you have? Do not even the tax-collectors do the same? And if you greet only your brothers and sisters, what more are you doing than others? Do not even the Gentiles do the same? Be perfect, therefore, as your heavenly Father is perfect" (Matthew 5:43-48).

So what is Jesus saying to us? It means that as disciples of Jesus celebrating Independence Day, we are called to love and pray for the members of ISIS, Al-Qaeda, and all enemies of America.

Writing those words turns my stomach. I feel fear and revulsion when I remember these fellow human beings who cause destruction and terror. But in my baptism I was sealed with the Holy Spirit and marked as Christ's own forever. And so I trust that over time, the grace of God and the practice of faith will settle my stomach as I offer these prayers. I hope so. Fear and revulsion never lead the way to peace.

What makes for peace? Though it has never yet been properly fulfilled, the words of the Declaration of Independence still stand strong (especially if a simple substitution of "people" for "men" is made):

We hold these truths to be self-evident, that all people are created equal, that they are endowed by their Creator with certain unalienable rights, that among these are life, liberty and the pursuit of happiness. That to secure these rights, governments are instituted among people, deriving their just powers from the consent of the governed.

Growing Christians

The equality of all people before God and the importance of participatory consent to democracy are core values I want to pass on to my children. Along with the sometimes-troubled story of our family, I will pass on the troubled history of our nation. But I also want my children to know that the ideals on which our nation was founded are fundamentally strong. What history asks of us is to help our nation grow closer to those ideals, generation by generation.

Although politics can turn my stomach, as a disciple of Jesus I am called to love my neighbor. That means engaging in politics, the decision-making process by which both my neighbor and I are governed.

It's been ninety years that the Episcopal Church has had Independence Day on our calendar of feasts. I am no longer disturbed by this reality; I am grateful. Our church has made me think through my observance in a new way. It is more meaningful, and that matters. We practice faith to challenge us, not just for comfort.

Respond

Reread the Declaration of Independence. Spend some time with this sentence: "We hold these truths to be self-evident, that all men [people] are created equal, that they are endowed by their Creator with certain unalienable Rights, that among these are Life, Liberty and the pursuit of Happiness."

Discuss what this means through the lens of our Christian faith. How does the Baptismal Covenant intersect with this proclamation? Have an honest discussion about ways in which the United States has lived into these words—and ways that it has failed. Explore some ideas about how each of you can be an active and responsible citizen guided by your faith.

Learn More

Proper Psalms, Lessons, and Prayers were first appointed for this national observance in the Proposed Prayer Book of 1786. They were deleted, however, by the General Convention of 1789, primarily as a result of the intervention of Bishop William White. Though himself a supporter of the American Revolution, he felt that the required observance was inappropriate, since the majority of the Church's clergy had, in fact, been loyal to the British crown.

Writing about the Convention which had called for the observance of the day throughout "this Church, on the fourth of July, for ever," White said, "The members of the convention seem to have thought themselves so established in their station of ecclesiastical legislators, that they might expect of the many clergy who had been averse to the American revolution the adoption of this service; although, by the use of it, they must make an implied acknowledgment of their error, in an address to Almighty God…The greater stress is laid on this matter because of the notorious fact, that the majority of the clergy could not have used the service, without subjecting themselves to ridicule and censure. For the author's part, having no hindrance of this sort, he contented himself with having opposed the measure, and kept the day from respect to the requisition of the convention; but could never hear of its being kept, in above two or three places beside Philadelphia." It was not until the revision of 1928 that provision was again made for the liturgical observance of the day.

Pray

Lord God Almighty, in whose Name the founders of this country won liberty for themselves and for us, and lit the torch of freedom for nations then unborn: Grant that we and all the people of this land may have grace to maintain our liberties in righteousness and peace; through Jesus Christ our Lord, who lives and reigns with you and the Holy Spirit, one God, for ever and ever. *Amen.*

Saint Mary Magdalene

Read

Psalm 42:1-7 | Judith 9:1, 11-14
2 Corinthians 5:14-18 | John 20:11-18

Reflect

Even though her eyes are swollen and sensitive from days of crying, her heart broken so that she feels she can hardly breathe, Mary Magdalene makes her way down the narrow, rocky path. I imagine her mind has raced toward this moment since she and her grief-stricken friends laid the body of her dead *Rabouni*, her teacher, in the tomb three days earlier. In her anxiety to get back to his body, to give it a real and sacred preparation for burial, she probably feels very overwhelmed. Not up to the task, perhaps, and out of her depth to be doing this important thing for the Son of God who has meant so much to her.

> ### Author
>
> **Heather Sleightholm** is an artist, wife, and mother living in northeastern Oklahoma.

Yet on the path that morning, the jar of herbs in her hands, she must realize that no matter how unqualified she feels, she is the only one showing up. If her Lord is to receive a proper burial, she is the only one approaching the tomb to see that it gets done. So she takes a deep breath and approaches the tomb. Then, miraculously, she hears him call her name.

For me, one of the most moving pieces of Jesus' resurrection is the fact that he chooses to first reveal himself to those who stayed with him to the end. The women, who have sat at his feet and wept as the apostles fled, are the ones who take him from the cross and the ones who return to make sure he is given a proper burial. They are the ones who stay and then return when things get hard. And to them he first reveals the triumph of his resurrection. He doesn't choose the Pharisees, or even the apostles, which might have made for a more blockbuster story. Instead he chooses the gentle workers who have shown up to quietly lay him to rest. He chooses the ones who *show up* and act out of their love for him, even when all seems lost.

There have been many situations in my own life where I felt like I was starting a journey into something that felt overwhelming—where I thought, "Surely there's someone more qualified than I am to do this." But the interesting thing about Jesus is that he isn't searching for the most qualified to do big things. He's looking for the willing and open-hearted.

On this Feast of Saint Mary Magdalene, I'd like to remind you— and myself—that we are all chosen for great things. No matter our family backgrounds, our past, our complicated relationships, our education (or lack there-of), our social standing, our orientation, or our gender, we are meant for great things. We just need to start down the path and listen for his voice.

Respond

Bake a special treat of magdalenas to honor Mary Magdalene. According to legend, a young Spanish girl named Madeleine (or Magdalena, depending on the legend) baked and served shell-shaped cakes (magdalenas) to pilgrims who traveled the Camino de Santiago. Search your cookbooks or online for a recipe.

While you're baking, talk with the members of your household about the calls to action you have heard from God—and the ways in which you think God might be calling them, too.

Learn More

Mary of Magdala, a town near Capernaum, was one of several women who followed Jesus and ministered to him in Galilee. The Gospel according to Luke records that Jesus "went on through cities and villages, preaching and bringing the good news of the kingdom of God. And the Twelve were with him, and also some women who had been healed of evil spirits and infirmities: Mary, called Magdalene, from whom seven demons had gone out…" (Luke 8:1-2). The gospels tell us that Mary was healed by Jesus, followed him, and was one of those who stood near his cross at Calvary.

It is clear that Mary Magdalene's life was radically changed by Jesus' healing. Her ministry of service and steadfast companionship, even as a witness to the crucifixion, has, through the centuries, been an example of the faithful ministry of women to Christ. All four gospels name Mary as one of the women who went to the tomb to mourn and to care for Jesus' body. Her weeping for the loss of her Lord strikes a common chord with the grief of all others over the death of loved ones. Jesus' tender response to her grief—meeting her in the garden, revealing himself to her by calling her name—makes her the first witness to the risen Lord. She is given the command, "Go to my brothers and say to them, 'I am ascending to my Father and your Father, to my God and your God'" (John 20:17). As the first messenger of the resurrection, she tells the disciples, "I have seen the Lord" (John 20:18).

In the tradition of the Eastern Church, Mary is considered "equal to the apostles" and "apostle to the apostles;" and she is held in veneration as the patron saint of the great cluster of monasteries on Mount Athos.

Pray

Almighty God, whose blessed Son restored Mary Magdalene to health of body and of mind, and called her to be a witness of his resurrection: Mercifully grant that by your grace we may be healed from all our infirmities and know you in the power of his unending life; Through the same Jesus Christ our Lord, who with you and the Holy Spirit lives and reigns, one God, now and for ever. *Amen.*

JULY **25**

Saint James the Apostle

Read

Psalm 7:1-10 | Jeremiah 45:1-5
Acts 11:27—12:3 | Matthew 20:20-28

Reflect

On this day, the Feast of Saint James, my thoughts and prayers are drawn to the practice of pilgrimage.

Nine years ago, I thought pilgrimage was a cool concept, and I had a list of destinations I hadn't yet reached.

Author

Christina (Tina) Clark lives in Denver, Colorado, has two teenage sons, and loves all things church, the Rocky Mountains, and the Pacific Ocean.

I had no idea what pilgrimage really meant.

Today, I'm getting there, and you may not realize it, but so are you.

In retrospect, this journey of life in faith is, every day, a pilgrimage. Each chapter in each of our stories describes a moment of striving, struggling, holding on, and letting go. It's only the ratios of each that change.

In 2013, I planned my first nominal pilgrimage for our high school youth. Along the way, I came to understand that in order to lead others on this sort of trip, I needed to grow my internal understanding of what it meant to be a pilgrim.

Like any devoted scholar of the twenty-first century, I turned to the internet. And found, much to my surprise, *Pilgrimage Magazine*, whose mission is to explore story, spirit, place, and witness in the American Southwest, which is where we would be traveling for our pilgrimage.

Four years later, our third high school pilgrimage just returned from eight days of story, spirit, and witness in some truly breathtaking places: the Canyon de Chelly, Monument Valley, the San Juan River, and Arches National Park in Moab, Utah. This journey, like the two before it, transformed teens and adult leaders alike. Our stories changed, not only to include all we experienced but also to add a renewed understanding of who we are, who we want to be, and how we interpret God's call to each of us.

The Spirit traveled with us, every step of the way. We took a group of teens who were anxious about being away from the familiar trappings of their daily lives: phones, friends, and possibly most worrying to them, showers. They struggled at first to let go and be fully present with themselves and one another. But through time and connection, by building relationships with our guides and our Navajo hosts, through the daily practice of morning and evening prayer, it all clicked into place one day, and there they were, fully immersed and present.

Pilgrimage presents us with the chance to explore our relationship with God and the world by literally changing the scenery and jarring us out of our everyday experience. Witness describes the reality that even in the mundane routines of our daily lives, we are pilgrims.

Today we celebrate Saint James, brother to John, son of Zebedee. We find James in some of the most critical moments of the gospel, including the Transfiguration and at Gethsemane. James and John, like Peter and Andrew just before them, are fishermen whom Jesus calls from their boat where they are mending nets with their father. And they drop the nets, leave their father, and follow Jesus (Matthew 4:21-22).

Reading the gospel, it is clear that James is by Jesus' side throughout his ministry. We glean that there is a deep friendship there, and James is witness to Christ's teachings, his miracles, his death, and resurrection. This is witness as most of us can only imagine.

After Jesus commissions the apostles, James makes his way to the Iberian Peninsula and spreads the good news in Spain. Eventually, he returns to Jerusalem, where he is slain at the command of Herod Agrippa I. He is the first of the twelve to be martyred. The story from there is that he is laid in a stone boat, which is carried by angels to the Atlantic coast of Spain and laid to rest in a tomb there. This is the place where pilgrims on the Santiago (Spanish for Saint James) de Compostela complete their journey.

I dream of someday making that pilgrimage. In the meantime, Saint James's example leads me to understand my place as a pilgrim at all times and in all places. My friendship, my witness to the stories of those around me, especially the "least of these," and my ministry to children and youth are all part of my own, lifelong pilgrimage.

It has been said: "We are spiritual beings having a human experience."

Every day of that experience is pilgrimage.

Respond

Consider taking a pilgrimage as a household. We often think of pilgrimages as journeys to faraway places steeped in holy histories, but they can also include visiting a nearby destination where you intentionally strive to connect with God. Research your community and see if there are places considered "pilgrimage destinations" nearby. If there's not a specific place, you might consider a cathedral, a monastic community, park, or retreat center. Check in with members of your household as you begin your journey by asking how they are feeling. When you arrive, invite God to walk with you on this pilgrimage and give you the patience to notice the little things. Where are your eyes drawn first? Where does your mind travel? Sit or walk in silence, considering what you see, hear, smell, and feel. Before you leave, come together with your family and offer a final prayer.

Learn More

James, the brother of John, is often known as James the Greater, to distinguish him from the other apostle of the same name who is commemorated on May 1 with Philip, and also from James "the brother of our Lord."

He was the son of a Galilean fisherman, Zebedee, and with his brother John left his home and his trade in obedience to the call of Christ. With Peter and John, he seems to have belonged to an especially privileged group, whom Jesus chose to be witnesses to the Transfiguration, to the raising of Jairus' daughter, and to his agony in the Garden of Gethsemane.

Apparently, James shared John's hot-headed disposition, and Jesus nicknamed the brothers, *Boanerges* (Sons of Thunder). James' expressed willingness to share the cup of Christ was realized in his being the first of the apostles to die for him.

As the Acts of the Apostles records, "About that time Herod the King laid violent hands upon some who belonged to the Church. He killed James the brother of John with the sword" (Acts 12:1-2).

According to an old tradition, the body of James was taken to Compostela, Spain, which has been a shrine for pilgrims for centuries.

Pray

O Gracious God, we remember before you today your servant and apostle James, first among the Twelve to suffer martyrdom for the Name of Jesus Christ; and we pray that you will pour out upon the leaders of your church that spirit of self-denying service by which alone they may have true authority among your people; through Jesus Christ our Lord, who lives and reigns with you and the Holy Spirit, one God, now and for ever. *Amen.*

AUGUST 6

The Transfiguration of Our Lord Jesus Christ

Read

Psalm 99 *or* 99:5-9 | Exodus 34:29-35
2 Peter 1:13-21 | Luke 9:28-36

Reflect

The Feast of the Transfiguration has always been a favorite of mine. My first preaching assignment in seminary was on Luke 9:28-36, the story of the Transfiguration. And from the beginning, I loved this story and all that it said about Jesus. I love to imagine Jesus revealed in all this glory, transfigured and shining like the sun. I love the way that the two greats of the Hebrew Bible, Moses and Elijah, appear next to Jesus, surrounding him with the great cloud of witnesses that have gone before. I love the part where the heavens are torn open, and the

Author
Melody Wilson Shobe and her husband, both Episcopal priests, and their two daughters live in Dallas, Texas. Melody spends her spare time reading stories, building forts, conquering playgrounds, baking cookies, and exploring nature.

voice of God thunders through the air: "This is my Son, the Beloved, listen to him!"

I have always loved this story, but I encountered this feast in a new and different way nine years ago. Because nine years ago, on the Feast of the Transfiguration, my daughter Isabelle was born.

It wasn't the day that she was supposed to come into the world. She was due on August 9, a Feria, a date when there is no feast in the Episcopal Church's calendar. But she had her own time (or, more rightly, God has God's own time), and the Feast of the Transfiguration became her natal feast. Every year on this great feast of our Lord, my family celebrates Isabelle. We give her gifts, we bake her cakes, we sing her happy birthday. And, of course, that is meet and right, because there is nothing I'd rather celebrate than this amazing, incredible person I get to know.

But here's the thing about that Feast of the Transfiguration nine years ago. It didn't just reveal Isabelle, in all her glory, to the world. It changed me forever. On this day nine years ago, I was transfigured; I was transformed and re-made. My entire identity shifted; I became a mom. It changed the way that I spend my time and spend my money and spend my energy. It changed who I am and how I relate to the world. It changed my body and my mind and my soul. Isabelle was the one who was born, who came into the world on this day, as the voice of God thundered in my ears: "This is my daughter, the Beloved." But I was the one who was transfigured.

So it was in my life, and so it is, I believe in all of ours. In fact, I think we learn this when we explore the biblical story. On the Feast of the Transfiguration, Jesus is transfigured: beautifully, powerfully, wonderfully. But he's not the only one. The disciples who see him fall to the ground with fear and trembling. Jesus is revealed to them in all his glory, and they (I have to imagine) are also transfigured, changed by what they see and know. The Jesus they see that day is burned onto their brains, burrowed into their lives, and they will never be the same.

That's how it should be with all of us. Jesus' transfiguration should transfigure and transform us. We should be just as changed by our encounter with the risen Lord as the disciples were on this day thousands of years ago. And we should be just as changed by our relationship with Jesus as we are by our encounters with the transfiguring people in our lives: our spouses, our children, our friends. In fact, "Christian" should be an even more transformative identity than "mother" or "father" or "spouse" or any of the other names and relationships by which we identify ourselves.

The transfigured Jesus should transfigure all of us, shifting our entire identities. It should change the way that we spend our time and spend our money and spend our energy. It should change who we are and how we relate to the world. It should change our bodies and our minds and our souls.

Respond

We learn in today's gospel reading that Jesus became dazzling white while on Mount Tabor with Peter, James, and John. Plan a meal today that centers around the color white. Decorate with a white tablecloth or napkins, light white candles, and serve white food and drinks such as potato soup, white cheddar macaroni and cheese, milk, or vanilla ice cream. While feasting on this dazzling white dinner, share stories about how you have been transfigured by people in your life.

Learn More

The Transfiguration is not to be understood only as a spiritual experience of Jesus while at prayer, which three chosen disciples, Peter, James, and John, were permitted to witness. It is one of a series of spiritual manifestations by which God authenticated Jesus as his Son. It is at one with the appearance of the angels at the birth and at his resurrection, and with the descent of the Spirit at Jesus' baptism.

Matthew records the voice from heaven saying, "This is my Son, the Beloved, with whom I am well pleased; listen to him!" (Matthew 17:5). Briefly the veil is drawn aside, and a chosen few are permitted to see Jesus, not only as the human son of Mary, but also as the eternal Son of God. Moses and Elijah witness to Jesus as the fulfillment of the Law and the Prophets. In Luke's account of the event, they speak of the "exodus" which Jesus is to accomplish at Jerusalem. A cloud, a sign of divine presence, envelops the disciples, and a heavenly voice proclaims Jesus to be the Son of God.

Immediately thereafter, Jesus announces to Peter, James, and John the imminence of his death. As Paul was later to say of Jesus, "Though he was in the form of God, did not regard equality with God as something to be exploited, but emptied himself, taking the form of a slave, being born in human likeness. And being found in human form, he humbled himself and became obedient to the point of death— even death on a cross" (Philippians 2:6-8).

The Feast of the Transfiguration is held in the highest esteem by the Eastern Churches. The figure of the transfigured Christ is regarded as a foreshadowing of the Risen and Ascended Lord. The festival, however, was only accepted into the Roman calendar on the eve of the Reformation, and for that reason was not originally included in the reformed calendar of the Church of England. Since its inclusion in the American liturgical revision of 1892, it has been taken into most modern Anglican calendars.

Pray

O God, who on the holy mount revealed to chosen witnesses your well-beloved Son, wonderfully transfigured, in raiment white and glistening: Mercifully grant that we, being delivered from the disquietude of this world, may by faith behold the King in his beauty; who with you, O Father, and you, O Holy Spirit, lives and reigns, one God, for ever and ever. *Amen.*

Growing Christians

AUGUST **15**

Saint Mary the Virgin, Mother of Our Lord Jesus Christ

Read

Psalm 34 *or* 34:1-9 | Isaiah 61:10-11
Galatians 4:4-7 | Luke 1:46-55

Reflect

I was trying to compose myself in a stairwell the first time Saint Mary the Virgin ever made sense to me.

It was Christmas Eve, the first one since I had lost my dad that July. The great big, beautiful church where I served on staff had a full evening's lineup of Christmas Eve services for the many people who would come to worship, whether they were Sunday regulars or just felt drawn to touch home base at a tender time of year. The choir had prepared piece after moving piece, familiar and new (if you think you're busy in December, talk to a church musician!). The

Author

Ann Benton Fraser, an Episcopal priest, lives with her husband Andrew and their three children in San Antonio, Texas. She spends time reading, being outside, and learning from her children.

rector had preached a sermon that shattered me in the best way, connecting me with the wonder—love!—of God made known to us in human form, in Jesus.

Family longings can be acute around holidays, and maybe that's why Mary as mother of Jesus came to me in that stairwell between services. I don't mean to say I had a vision, but more of a knowing: an assurance that wherever my dad was in death, it had to do with where Mary was, too. *Nearer, my God, to thee.*

Episcopalians don't always know how to regard Mary; there's a wide spectrum of thought, belief, and practice when it comes to ideas like the virgin birth of Jesus or praying to a saint. Traditions about Mary have developed over the centuries, beyond and apart from what we find in scripture. What is vital to some is puzzling to others; motherhood and sexuality are powerful and complex parts of human nature. Sometimes it seems like popular theology peels off feminine attributes of God and sticks them on Mary—making too little of God and too much of Mary.

Jesus is the mediator between God and humanity—we already have a Holy One who bridges for us the human and divine. Like all the saints, though, Mary can point us to God, drawing us in. Saints—those faithful believers of ages past—can give us real-life examples of what it is to follow our Lord. We are enlightened by learning how others lived their faith in their time and place. Seeing other saints, we are encouraged to let the gospel direct us in our own context.

But there is something about Mary.

Mary is unique in her role as mother of our Lord; she is sometimes called *Theotokos*, God-bearer. The gospels give us wonderful glimpses of Mary's courage in saying yes to the invitation of God. Right from the start, the angel addresses Mary as "favored one" in Luke's annunciation story.

My favorite portrayal of Mary comes from author Barbara Cawthorne Crafton's *Mary and Her Miracle*. Young Mary is climbing in the branches of a favorite tree when she has an experience of this message from God. She consents to God's plan for her to bring Jesus into the world, though it brings more questions than answers. That is right in line with our gospel-tellers, too. Luke takes the time to mention Mary's interior life when the shepherds come with angel-chorus stories to greet the newborn Jesus: "Mary treasured these words and pondered them in her heart."

What would it mean to be mother to this child?

When the baby was presented in the temple, the Spirit-led Simeon "blessed them and said to his mother Mary, 'This child is destined for the falling and the rising of many in Israel...and a sword will pierce your own soul too'" (Luke 2:34-35).

In John's Gospel, we find Mary standing near the cross where her son is being crucified, as Jesus commends her to the care of his beloved disciple. Art has sought to express the pain of the mother with the sword-pierced soul in the *pietá*, the image of Mary cradling her son Jesus after his death.

Not every image and traditional tale of Mary speaks to my soul. But I am moved by the willing courage of a young person saying yes to God's adventure.

Can I consent to God being born in me, brought to others and made known in my life? I find the grief of a mother compelling, and—given my stairwell blessing, I discovered that grief to be full of grace and hope. I'm grateful for a church rhythm that visits and revisits the holy stories of that nearer-to-God way of being. And I'm grateful for Mary, still bearing God to us.

Respond

Say Evening Prayer together (found in *The Book of Common Prayer*, starting on page 115). Pay particular attention to the *Magnificat*, or the Song of Mary. This hymn (from Luke 1:46-55) is a glorious song of praise. It has been set to music by choirs through the ages. Search online for various recordings. Talk with each other about what it might mean for your soul to magnify the Lord.

Learn More

The honor paid to Mary, the Mother of Jesus Christ, goes back to the earliest days of the church. Two gospels tell of the manner of Christ's birth, and the familiar Christmas story testifies to the church's conviction that he was born of a virgin. In Luke's Gospel, we catch a brief glimpse of Jesus' upbringing at Nazareth, when the child was in the care of his mother and her husband Joseph.

During Jesus' ministry in Galilee, we learn that Mary was often with the other women who followed Jesus and ministered to his needs. At Calvary, she was among the little band of disciples who kept watch at the cross. After the resurrection, she was to be found with the Twelve in the upper room, watching and praying until the coming of the Spirit at Pentecost.

Mary was the person closest to Jesus in his most impressionable years, and the words of the Magnificat, as well as her courageous acceptance of God's will, bear more than an accidental resemblance to the Lord's Prayer and the Beatitudes of the Sermon on the Mount.

Later devotion has claimed many things for Mary beyond the brief description that is given in Holy Scripture. What we can believe is that one who stood in so intimate a relationship with the incarnate Son of God on earth must, of all human beings, have the place of highest honor in the eternal life of God. A paraphrase of an ancient Greek hymn expresses this belief in very familiar words: "O higher than the cherubim, more glorious than the seraphim, lead their praises, alleluia."

Pray

O God, you have taken to yourself the blessed Virgin Mary, mother of your incarnate Son: Grant that we, who have been redeemed by his blood, may share with her the glory of your eternal kingdom; through Jesus Christ our Lord, who lives and reigns with you, in the unity of the Holy Spirit, one God, now and for ever. *Amen.*

Saint Bartholomew the Apostle

Read

Psalm 91 *or* 91:1-4 | Deuteronomy 18:15-18
1 Corinthians 4:9-15 | Luke 22:24-30

Reflect

"Who empties the trash, Daddy?"

We were standing in front of an overflowing trash can in a neighborhood fast-food chicken franchise. It took me a moment to register my son asking me the question. I'd been daydreaming and lost in thought. Again.

Returning to the present moment, I quickly became elbow deep in a trash can filled with discarded cups,

Author

Ben Day, an Episcopal priest, is an avid reader, cyclist, and runner and single father to a young son, Marshall. They live in Kennesaw, Georgia.

wrappers, half-eaten food, and other kinds of refuse left only to the imagination, trying to compact the garbage to make room for the mountain I needed to cram in on top. It was a sobering return to reality, a flashing symbol of where my whole life stood at that moment, much as I tried to summarily reject and forget the symbolic connections flooding my mind.

The distracted daydreaming didn't begin at the trash can. I had spent much of that meal distracted, lost in thought and self-pity. If I'm to be rigorously honest, it wasn't just that meal, either, but all the ones that preceded it for weeks now, maybe even months. I was losing track of how long it had been since I was fully present around a table of food.

Mealtime brought into sharp relief the loneliness, pain, and loss of divorce. My son's mother and my former spouse is an excellent chef, a real self-taught gourmet. Throughout our relationship, we regularly prepared and consumed lavish meals together, enjoying the communion of one another's company alongside the culinary products of our labor. Her absence felt heaviest around mealtimes now. In an attempt to avoid the unpleasant feelings that come with separation, I stopped cooking almost entirely in the weeks and months following her moving out.

Fast food offered a change of scenery from our kitchen full of memories. It is also cheap, efficient, and concentrated time with my son, I told myself by way of justification. If I stayed focused on him, and avoided all places and rituals that reminded me of her or the family unit now lost in litigation and estrangement, my heartbreak and loneliness would stop. That was the plan, anyway.

Here I was again, lost in a daydream. Now elbow deep in trash trying to force more space in the world in which to pile more trash. It sounded an awful lot like the last days of my marriage.

Growing Christians

Distraction, avoidance, and willfulness—those words came up a lot in emergency couples counseling. They came up a lot in court-ordered mediation to settle the details of a temporary custody agreement and other exigencies of the one becoming two again.

Surprise! Here they were again.

"Who empties the trash, Daddy?"
"I don't know," I said, "Who do you think it is?"
"God knows," he said.
"Oh yeah?" I said
"Yep! It's probably somebody big and strong like you, Daddy" he said. "I am still too little, taking out the trash means you have to be big and brave!"

In silence, I thought to myself about strength, bravery, and my capacity to "take out the trash" of pain, heartbreak, and loneliness in my own life. To heal, I would need these skills and attributes. Was I up to it? Was I big and brave enough? My son didn't have a clue that his words were ringing in my heart or that his imaginative job description for the work of clearing trash was actually a challenge to my present situation.

Today is the Feast of Saint Bartholomew. Despite brief honorable mentions in each of the synoptic gospels, and a scholastically sketchy conflation with Nathanael in the first chapter of John's Gospel, we know very little about this apostle and saint. Tradition holds that he met a grisly martyr's death after helping found the Church in Armenia but little else is recorded of his life or ministry.

Yet, even in the absence of a robust account of his life or ministry, Bartholomew's feast day is celebrated as one of the major feasts of the church in equal standing and prominence as fellow apostles whose lives and ministries are better understood and recorded (ie: Peter, John, or Paul).

In celebrating this feast, we hold his significance as an unseen matter of faith. While largely unknown in modernity, Bartholomew's life was certainly consequential and significant among those he met, taught, and influenced as apostle and witness to the resurrected Christ in the first century. That's all we know about him.

Who empties the trash, Daddy? Who is Saint Bartholomew? These questions resemble one another, and their answers require filling in gaps from circumstantial evidence and context clues.

Neither my son nor I know the name of the worker who empties the trash, but my son knows you have to be big and strong to do it. He knows that you have to use your strength to be brave. We imagined together what it might be like to have that job, and having determined the qualifications, he was pretty sure I was up to the task, too.

As a community of believers celebrating his feast day, we do not know many details of Bartholomew's life and ministry, but as an apostle called by Christ and as a witness to his resurrected life, we know his life to be one of profound significance and sacrificial service. After all, it led to his death among the martyrs of our faith.

In both cases, we seek to determine what we do not know, and in both cases, gratitude rises in our hearts from what we can surmise or imagine.

A year after the trash can incident, my son and I have developed a regular pattern of imaginative inquiry conversations about all manner of topics.

We talk about the sprinkles on his Saturday morning doughnut: who is the sugarcane farmer, the wheat grower, the pastry chef who prepared his treat?

We talk about the landscaping in the park around the corner from our house: who planted the seeds, cleared the flowerbed, mulched and cultivated the ground, and made it beautiful?

We talk about the firefighters who are always washing their bright red truck when we pass their station on the commute to daycare. Who might need them today? People who are sick? People who are building new houses and need them inspected? Little boys and girls who need to learn what to do in an emergency?

Lately, we even talk about my work as a parish priest. He likes to imagine what I do all day while he is at daycare, and I let his imagination run wild because often it's way cooler than what is actually scheduled on my calendar.

Each brief wondering forces us to take notice of the circumstances and small context clues in our world. Moreover, they force us to go deep and approach the people and items that populate our lives with gratitude and carefulness.

I knew this practice was working when at a fourth birthday party for a classmate, my son went up to the mom of the honoree holding his cupcake and said, "Thank you for the cake and for the farmers, gardeners, and cake makers who helped you." She looked over at me and made eye contact with a smile, then looked back at my son standing beneath her, took his hand, and said, "Thank you for coming here to celebrate, and for your daddy who drove you, the car mechanic who tuned up your car so it runs smoothly, and the refinery worker who produced the gasoline in the engine." He beamed!

Respond

Spend some time with the concept of imaginative inquiry. How can you get children and teens involved in wondering aloud about those who populate their lives, seen and unseen, known and unknown?

Who stocks the grocery store shelves? Who paves the roads? What does your priest do during the week? What might the ministry of a store clerk be? Who should we thank for cupcakes and swimming pools and our favorite music?

Learn More

Bartholomew is one of the twelve apostles known in the gospels according to Matthew, Mark, and Luke only by name. His name means "Son of Tolmai," and he is sometimes identified with Nathanael, the friend of Philip, the "Israelite without guile" in John's Gospel, to whom Jesus promised the vision of angels ascending and descending on the Son of Man.

There is a tradition that Bartholomew traveled to India, and Eusebius reports that when Pantaenus of Alexandria visited India, between 150 and 200, he found there "the Gospel according to Matthew" in Hebrew, which had been left behind by "Bartholomew, one of the Apostles."

An ancient tradition maintains that Bartholomew was flayed alive at Albanopolis in Armenia.

Pray

Almighty and everlasting God, who gave to your apostle Bartholomew grace truly to believe and to preach your Word: Grant that your church may love what he believed and preach what he taught; through Jesus Christ our Lord, who lives and reigns with you and the Holy Spirit, one God, for ever and ever. *Amen.*

SEPTEMBER 15

Holy Cross Day

Read

Psalm 98 *or* 98:1-4 | Isaiah 45:21-25
Philippians 2:5-11 *or* Galatians 6:14-18 | John 12:31-36a

Reflect

As we reach the middle of September, we also reach Holy Cross Day. Holy Cross Day is a major feast day in the Episcopal Church with ancient roots but was only added to our liturgical calendar in 1979. The feast of the Holy Cross can be found in both the Orthodox and Roman Catholic traditions and traces its beginning back to the fourth century. The feast of the Holy Cross, also known as "the exultation of the Holy Cross" and "The Triumph of the Cross," celebrates Christ's self-offering on the cross for our salvation but in a more joyful context outside the somber atmosphere of Lent.

Author

Heather Sleightholm is an artist, wife, and mother living in northeastern Oklahoma.

Over the summer, I had the great opportunity to train as a catechist for the Montessori-based faith formation program, Catechesis of the Good Shepherd. In my studies, I learned

Growing Christians

that our main goal for children in their beginning years is to make them fall in love with their shepherd, Jesus, and to find great joy and comfort in their faith. When speaking of the crucifixion, it is always followed by his resurrection, so that the joy of the moment of triumph is the focus—not suffering.

This concept has greatly helped me as a mother of young children, because I often feel at a loss for words when trying to explain the crucifixion in the midst of the sorrow of Lent. Holy Cross Day offers us a more joyful and instantly triumphant opportunity to introduce the concept of Jesus and the cross to little ones by celebrating the meaning of the sacrifice instead of concentrating on the painful process of it.

According to the *Lesser Feasts and Fasts* of the Episcopal Church, the collect for this Holy Day reads,

> Almighty God, whose Son our Savior Jesus Christ was lifted high upon the cross that he might draw the whole world unto himself; Mercifully grant that we, who glory in the mystery of our redemption, may have grace to take up our cross and follow him; who liveth and reigneth with thee and the Holy Spirit, One God, in glory everlasting. *Amen.*

This passage would be a wonderful prayer to read at the dinner table or during a quiet part of the evening and muse about with your child. Some questions to ask may include, "What is a cross? What does it look like? Why is it a special symbol?"

Of course, when asking questions to children under the age of seven, we are mostly posing the questions for them to mull over instead of giving concrete answers. However, you might find yourself bowled over by the answer you get!

At church on Holy Cross Day, you might decide to go on a bit of treasure hunt to see where you can spot a cross within the building or on the church grounds. This is a wonderful opportunity to explain to your child that the cross is the sign of Jesus and for Christians, a sign of blessing.

Expanding on that idea, Holy Cross Day offers a chance to explain the holy water font near the door of the church or within your own home. Show your child how to make the sign of the cross. Let them know that when we make this gesture, we are marking ourselves as blessed by God because of Jesus' sacrifice on the cross. And when we see the priest make this sign in front of the whole church, the priest is blessing everyone in the room.

If you're in the mood for some merry-making, make a batch of hot cross buns or decorate the top of a cake—or even a pizza, quiche, lasagna, anything really, with a cross. This is not a day with a set of concrete rules for how to celebrate.

Regardless of how you mark the day, I think it's a perfect occasion to gently introduce your child to the Holy Cross, the sign of the cross, and why this symbol is meaningful to their church and family. The children may not have the words to articulate much about the cross, but they will listen and internalize. Therefore, it is important that we teach them early about how the cross is a sign of love and blessing and how to use it within their everyday life.

Respond

Get crafty together. Make a simple holy cross pillow that will be a reminder for many days to come of the power and love of the cross. Episcopal evangelist Jerusalem Jackson Greer offers instructions for this craft in her book, *A Homemade Year: The Blessings of Cooking, Crafting, and Coming Together.* Also available online at catholicmom.com

Learn More

The historian Eusebius, in his *Life of Constantine*, tells how that emperor ordered the erection of a complex of buildings in Jerusalem "on a scale of imperial magnificence," to set forth as "an object of attraction and veneration to all, the blessed place of our Savior's resurrection." The overall supervision of the work—on the site where the Church of the Holy Sepulchre now stands—was entrusted to Constantine's mother, the empress Helena.

In Jesus' time, the hill of Calvary had stood outside the city; but when the Roman city that succeeded Jerusalem, Aelia Capitolina, was built, the hill was buried under tons of fill. It was during the excavations directed by Helena that a relic, believed to be that of the true cross, was discovered.

Constantine's shrine included two principal buildings: a large basilica, used for the Liturgy of the Word, and a circular church, known as "The Resurrection"—its altar placed on the site of the tomb—which was used for the Liturgy of the Table, and for the singing of the Daily Office.

Toward one side of the courtyard which separated the two buildings, and through which the faithful had to pass on their way from Word to Sacrament, the exposed top of Calvary's hill was visible. It was there that the solemn veneration of the cross took place on Good Friday; and it was there that the congregation gathered daily for a final prayer and dismissal after Vespers.

The dedication of the buildings was completed on September 14, 335, the seventh month of the Roman calendar, a date suggested by the account of the dedication of Solomon's temple in the same city, in the seventh month of the Jewish calendar, hundreds of years before (2 Chronicles 7:8-10).

Pray

Almighty God, whose Son our Savior Jesus Christ was lifted high upon the cross that he might draw the whole world to himself: Mercifully grant that we, who glory in the mystery of our redemption, may have grace to take up our cross and follow him; who lives and reigns with you and the Holy Spirit, one God, in glory everlasting. *Amen.*

Saint Matthew, Apostle and Evangelist

Read

Psalm 119:33-40 | Proverbs 3:1-6
2 Timothy 3:14-17 | Matthew 9:9-13

Reflect

Saturdays have never really been a day for our family to sleep in.

Between sports, church life, hiking trips, and other adventures, we are typically up and moving on Saturdays. However, this does not prevent a protest from the children, especially when we have to get up early.

My previous parish served one Saturday morning per month with a ministry called Feed Thy Neighbor hosted at St. Andrew's Episcopal Church in Greenville, South Carolina. Episcopal parishes in Greenville partner together in a joint ministry to provide breakfast on Saturdays to the homeless and working poor. Feed

Author

Dorian Del Priore is an Episcopal priest who has been involved in youth ministry for more than twenty years. Dorian is a husband to Lauren and a father to Jordan and Brynn, and they live in Columbia, South Carolina.

Thy Neighbor had two shifts, and the food prep shift required us to be up at 5:30 a.m. The second shift came in for cleanup. The team of roughly eight volunteers would prepare eggs, biscuits, sausage, and a huge pot of grits for about 100 people. Our team was always a mix of families, singles, and retirees, and it was a joyful, fun kitchen.

On one particular Saturday, my son Jordan was asked to greet at the door, handing out meal tickets. Jordan spent the whole morning in conversation with many of these new friends. One of the regulars was an older gentleman who always came dressed in a tie and blazer. Whether he was talkative by nature or just needed someone to talk to that morning, he talked Jordan's ear off. I could hear their laughter from the kitchen.

"Why does your teacher eat with tax collectors and sinners?"

The gospel passage for today, the Feast of Saint Matthew, is Matthew 9:9-13. Jesus calls Matthew, "Follow me." Matthew drops everything and follows immediately. Quickly the story shifts, and we find Jesus eating dinner with tax collectors and sinners.

The Pharisees are trying to call out Jesus for hanging with a less than respectable crowd. Publicans, like Matthew, were Jews who collaborated with the Roman Empire, collecting taxes and such, and they were particularly detested. They were so abhorred and outcast that many parents would not allow marriage into a family of which a publican was even a member. Someone like Matthew would cast a shadow, a stain, on the rest of the family.

Growing Christians

Jesus sees people differently, though. Jesus looks past the circumstances of a person and sees the person for who they truly are: beloved and bearing the image and likeness of God. And if Jesus truly sees each person in that way, what option does Jesus have but to eat with sinners? When Jesus sits down for dinner with tax collectors and sinners, Jesus performs a healing miracle, much like the healings of the paralytic, the hemorrhaging woman, blind Bartimaeus, and the ten lepers. True healing is about more than the physical. The deeper healing that Jesus brings about draws them back into community and relationship.

In some ways, this is a foreshadowing of the dinner at Emmaus. When we sit down and eat with one another, break bread together, Jesus is revealed to us. When we sit down and eat with one another, we are sharing a meal with Jesus. We participate in the reconciling work of Jesus. When we share a meal, we participate in the healing work of Jesus. "Those who are well have no need of a physician, but those who are sick."

Jesus closes with a stunning statement: "I desire mercy, not sacrifice. For I have come to call not the righteous but sinners." Is this exclusionary? Or is it an invitation to the table? Recognizing our brokenness, our necessary response to God's mercy is to hear the invitation of Jesus, "Follow me." We are healed ourselves when we participate in the healing work of Jesus.

When volunteering at a soup kitchen, food bank, or similar ministry of mercy, age-appropriate safety measures should and must be taken, but these ministries are perfectly accessible to families. Ministries such as Feed Thy Neighbor are powerful and transformative for young people and families. God is broken open and revealed to us in new and different ways. Our fear and judgment of the other withers, and we develop a greater capacity for compassion and grace.

I once read that we learn to love God by loving other people. One way we learn to love another is by sharing a meal with them. Whether at a soup kitchen or at a dinner party, at dinner with the church youth group or at the table of Holy Eucharist, we partner with and fully experience God's healing when we break bread together.

My prayer this Feast of Saint Matthew is that we will always listen for and respond to the invitation of Jesus: follow me.

Respond

Have your household research some of the local soup kitchens and food pantries. Select one that seems to need your help and call ahead to arrange a time to volunteer. You might consider committing to volunteering each week for a month so that your household might embrace this ministry as a habit, rather than a one-time special event.

Learn More

Matthew, one of Jesus' disciples, is probably to be identified with Levi, a tax collector ("publican") mentioned by Mark and Luke. In the Gospel according to Matthew, it is said that Matthew was seated in the custom-house when Jesus invited him, "Follow me." When Jesus called him, he at once left everything, followed Jesus, and later gave a dinner for him. Mark and Luke also note that Levi was a tax collector. In all three accounts, Jesus is severely criticized for eating at the same table with tax collectors and other disreputable persons.

Tax collectors were viewed as collaborators with the Roman State, extortioners who took money from their own people to further the cause of Rome and to line their own pockets. They were spurned as traitors and outcasts. The Jews so abhorred them that pious Pharisees refused to marry into a family that had a publican as a member. Clearly, Matthew was hardly the type of man that a devout Jew would have had among his closest associates. Yet Jesus noted that it was the publican rather than the proud Pharisee who prayed the acceptable prayer, "Lord, be merciful to me, a sinner." There are several favorable references to publicans in the sayings of Jesus in the Gospel according to Matthew.

According to the early Christian writers Irenaeus and Clement of Alexandria, Matthew converted many people to Christianity in Judea, and then traveled on to the East; however, there is no certain evidence for this. He has traditionally been venerated as a martyr, but the time and circumstances of his death are unknown.

Pray

We thank you, heavenly Father, for the witness of your apostle
and evangelist Matthew to the Gospel of your Son our Savior;
and we pray that, after his example, we may with ready wills
and hearts obey the calling of our Lord to follow him; through
Jesus Christ our Lord, who lives and reigns with you and the
Holy Spirit, one God, now and for ever. *Amen.*

Saint Michael and All Angels

Read

Psalm 103 *or* 103:19-22 | Genesis 28:10-17
Revelation 12:7-12 | John 1:47-51

Reflect

The New Testament names two angels: Gabriel and Michael. Michael has had greater historical devotion, thus today's feast Michaelmas or The Feast of Saint Michael and All Angels. Even with Michael's popularity, I wonder if the modern church isn't more comfortable with Gabriel. The difference might be obvious: Gabriel, who appears in the birth narratives, is the one who carries the message. Though terrifying in appearance ("Fear not"), Gabriel's holy task is a comfortable one: proclaim the good news.

Author

Patrick Funston, an Episcopal priest in Kansas, is husband to Michael, father to Eirnín and York, and an avid gamer and geek.

Michael's holy task is less comfortable: Warrior, Supreme Commander of the Heavenly Hosts, Five-Star General of God's Army.

When you see a representation of Michael the Archangel as described in scripture, do you see yourself?

I have trouble seeing myself. When I think of warriors, I often don't count myself among them. In the modern archetype, I'm not a warrior. I've never put on a uniform to serve in the military; I've never gone into battle. Michael, the patron saint of warriors, is undoubtedly the patron of those brave warriors who have given of themselves to this task. In the collect for today, we ask God that "by your appointment [angels] may help and defend us." These modern warriors will be on my mind.

But could Michael be my patron saint too?

When I was baptized, my parents and godparents promised on my behalf to "persevere in resisting evil" and to "strive for justice and peace." In countless baptisms since, I have affirmed my commitment to that work.

Persevere.

Strive.

These are warrior words.

In baptism formation, it's easy for us to lift up the profundity of the Baptismal Covenant and reinforce those questions over and over. They are wonderful and they are beautiful, but sometimes we gloss over another set of baptismal questions: our baptismal renunciations.

- Do you renounce Satan and all the spiritual forces of wickedness that rebel against God?

- Do you renounce the evil powers of this world which corrupt and destroy the creatures of God?

- Do you renounce all sinful desires that draw you from the love of God?

Our promise to "persevere in resisting evil," that against which we "strive for justice and peace," has already been described. Evil has three manifestations: Spiritual Forces of Wickedness, Evil Systems of this World, and the Sin Within.

Warriors don't have to carry weapons or wear armor. Any of us, living into our baptism, are warriors. Our modern dragons are put down by you and me and by thousands of others who fight the struggle against evil. When we acknowledge and repent of the sin within us, we are warriors. When we stand up to injustice, degradation, and exploitation, we are warriors.

Respond

Talk to your children about those who persevere and strive and tell stories of family and friends. What corruption and injustice do your children see? Pray for the strength to fight and brainstorm action appropriate to their age.

Pray for service members and for those speaking out and standing up to our modern cornucopia of domestic injustice. Pray that God's will be done and that peace and justice reign.

Write to your family's warriors. The word angel comes from the Greek, ἄγγελος, meaning messenger. Be an angel to a warrior, and send a message of love, hope, peace, and gratitude

Learn More

The biblical word "angel" (Greek: *angelos*) means, literally, a messenger. Messengers from God can be visible or invisible, and may assume human or nonhuman forms. Christians have always felt themselves to be attended by helpful spirits—swift, powerful, and enlightening. Those beneficent spirits are often depicted in Christian art in human form, with wings to signify their swiftness and spacelessness, with swords to signify their power, and with dazzling raiment to signify their ability to enlighten. Unfortunately, this type of pictorial representation has led many to dismiss the angels as "just another mythical beast, like the unicorn, the griffin, or the sphinx."

Of the many angels spoken of in the Bible, only four are called by name: Michael, Gabriel, Uriel, and Raphael. The Archangel Michael is the powerful agent of God who wards off evil from God's people, and delivers peace to them at the end of this life's mortal struggle. "Michaelmas," as his feast is called in England, has long been one of the popular celebrations of the Christian year in many parts of the world.

Michael is the patron saint of countless churches, including Mont Saint-Michel, the monastery fortress off the coast of Normandy that figured so prominently in medieval English history, and Coventry Cathedral, England's most famous modern church building, rising from the ashes of the Second World War.

Pray

Everlasting God, who has ordained and constituted in a wonderful order the ministries of angels and mortals: Mercifully grant that, as your holy angels always serve and worship you in heaven, so by your appointment they may help and defend us here on earth; through Jesus Christ our Lord, who lives and reigns with you and the Holy Spirit, one God, for ever and ever. *Amen.*

Saint Luke the Evangelist

Read

Psalm 147 *or* 147:1-7 | Ecclesiasticus 38:1-4
2 Timothy 4:5-13 | Luke 4:14-21

Reflect

Several years ago, the church I currently serve decided to end their Wednesday healing service, opting instead to add healing prayers to the Sunday morning liturgy. I learned about it during my interviews when it was made very clear that this was a sacred tradition (albeit a new one) that was going to stick around. I began working at this church last month and each Sunday I must be intentional about including these prayers. I'm so used to moving straight from the post-communion prayer to the final blessing that on my first Sunday, I forgot it all together... and then heard about it during coffee hour. The following week I made notes in my personal *Book of Common Prayer* and the altar book reminding me to invite people forward for anointing and laying on of hands.

Author

Allison Sandlin Liles is a wife, mother, peacemaker, and priest learning how to navigate life in the suburban wilds of Dallas, Texas.

Those who desire this sacrament stand before me for anointing while surrounding church members lay on hands. One week no one came up; other weeks a couple of folks await anointing. The Sunday after Dr. Christine Blasey Ford and Judge Brett Kavanaugh testified before the Senate, we had a record number of people seek healing. One of those people was my seven-year-old daughter.

The woman seated next to her on the front row invited her to lay hands on a gentleman who came forward. My daughter cautiously stood up, took a few steps, and gently touched his arm. Then she laid hands on the woman next in line. And then, she stepped in front of me, looked up, and asked to be anointed.

This was only my daughter's third Sunday at this new church. The first week, she and my son behaved beautifully. The second week, not so much. That week I shot her you-better-start-behaving laser beams out of my eyeballs while preaching. This third week, my son decided to sing with the choir, and my daughter set up shop on the back row with a stack of books. Then during the prelude, two people she didn't know sat down on either side of her, and she fled to the sacristy. When she finally returned during the epistle reading, she walked to the front row and sat down so close to me that we could have held hands.

Like me, she's still finding her way in this new church community. But something big happened during those healing prayers. She connected with fellow members while touching their arms and their hands touching her shoulders. After church, she told me how fun it was praying for people who felt sick and then being prayed for herself. I caught her smiling in the mirror once we got home, checking to see if the oil she could still feel on her forehead was visible. The following week as I placed the communion host in her small hands, she asked me if she could also get the oil and blessing. Soon, I told her. Right after our thank you prayer.

Today is the Feast of Saint Luke the Evangelist, the person attributed to writing the biblical books of Luke and Acts. Luke is often described as a physician because of Colossians 4:14 where the author relays that "Luke, the beloved physician, sends his greetings."

Physicians rely so heavily on their hands to detect problems in our bodies. Jesus relied heavily on his hands for healing people during his time on earth. On this feast day, I'm reminded of the role our hands also play in the sacraments of our church. Clergy touch the water in baptism, the bread during the eucharist, join the hands of couples getting married. Hands are laid upon the head for confirmation, ordination, and also upon those seeking healing.

Respond

A way to celebrate the Feast of Saint Luke today is to prayerfully lay your own hands on members of your household. You can hold a service of healing prayer and it need not be long or even formal. After dinner tonight, open with a prayer acknowledging God's presence in your midst. Ask those gathered to share something that's troubling them like an illness or school assignment or friendship or something at work. Then lay hands upon each other's head, shoulders, or arms, and take turns saying a prayer to ask God for healing.

Learn More

According to tradition, Luke was a physician and one of Paul's fellow missionaries in the early spread of Christianity throughout the Roman world. He has been identified as the writer of both the gospel that bears his name, and its sequel, the Acts of the Apostles.

Luke seems to have either been a Gentile or a Hellenistic Jew and, like the other New Testament writers, he wrote in Greek, so that Gentiles might learn about the Lord whose life and deeds so impressed him. In the first chapter of his gospel, he makes clear that he is offering authentic information about Jesus' birth, ministry, death, and resurrection, as it had been handed down to him from those who had firsthand knowledge.

Only Luke provides the very familiar stories of the annunciation to Mary, of her visit to Elizabeth, of the child in the manger, the angelic host appearing to shepherds, and the meeting with the aged Simeon. Luke also includes in his work six miracles and eighteen parables not recorded in the other gospels. In Acts he tells about the coming of the Holy

Spirit, the struggles of the apostles and their triumphs over persecution, of their preaching of the Good News, and of the conversion and baptism of other disciples, who would extend the church in future years.

Luke was with Paul apparently until the latter's martyrdom in Rome. What happened to Luke after Paul's death is unknown, but early tradition has it that he wrote his gospel in Greece, and that he died at the age of eighty-four in Boeotia.

Gregory of Nazianzus says that Luke was martyred, but this testimony is not corroborated by other sources. In the fourth century, the Emperor Constantius ordered the relics of Luke to be removed from Boeotia to Constantinople, where they could be venerated by pilgrims.

According to Orthodox Christian tradition, Luke was also the first iconographer. He is traditionally regarded as the patron saint of artists and physicians.

Pray

Almighty God, who inspired your servant Luke the physician to set forth in the Gospel the love and healing power of your Son: Graciously continue in your church this love and power to heal, to the praise and glory of your Name; through Jesus Christ our Lord, who lives and reigns with you, in the unity of the Holy Spirit, one God, now and for ever. *Amen.*

Saint James of Jerusalem, Brother of Our Lord Jesus Christ, and Martyr

Read

Psalm 1 | Acts 15:12-22a
1 Corinthians 15:1-11 | Matthew 13:54-58

Reflect

"Oh, you're So-and-So's sister!"

There are, perhaps, no more daunting and deflating words that any sibling can hear. They are an immediate sign that the person to whom you are speaking is already assessing and evaluating you— over and against the pattern of your sibling. For better or for worse, you will forever be defined by comparison.

I'm the oldest of three sisters, and I know my younger siblings dreaded these words from

Author
Melody Wilson Shobe and her husband, both Episcopal priests, and their two daughters live in Dallas, Texas. Melody spends her spare time reading stories, building forts, conquering playgrounds, baking cookies, and exploring nature.

teachers, who first had me in class, then each of them in turn. My sisters knew from the start that they wouldn't have a blank slate; they were always being held in comparison to some standard that I had set. As the quiet introvert, in contrast to my much more popular and extroverted sisters, I heard these comparisons often enough myself. They were usually accompanied by confusion about how different we are—my dark hair to their blonde, my nerdiness to their popularity. But occasionally there was also surprise about our similarities— phrases and mannerisms that we share, inside jokes based on beloved movies or memories that tied us together in a deep and unbreakable way.

As hard as that lifetime of comparison is for all siblings, it might have been hardest of all for James of Jerusalem, whose feast we celebrate today. "Oh, you're Jesus' brother!" he would have heard, his entire life.

And in those words were layer upon layer of meaning.

- "Oh, you're the brother of God incarnate!" said with hushed reverence.

- "Oh, you're the brother of the man who claims he's God!" said with scorn and disdain.

- "Oh, you're the brother of the man who makes the lame walk and the blind see!" said with the implied addition of "And what have you done lately?"

- "Oh, you're the brother of the man who teaches with astonishing authority and knowledge?" said with a quizzical intonation.

Growing Christians

If anyone, in the history of the world had a reason to resent his brother, it was James, the brother of Jesus. And yet, that's not what happened. Oh, it wasn't all smooth sailing. James did not follow Jesus in his lifetime, and he was not there by his side when his brother died. But James became one of the pillars of the church, preaching and spreading the gospel like wildfire. James became a saint in his own right, converting people to Christianity, praying for them diligently, serving them faithfully.

James was dedicated to his brother without being completely defined by him. He found a way not to resent his brother for who he was and who he wasn't but to embrace both his brother's identity and his own call. He was not Jesus and never could be. But he was James, and he could serve God as who he was.

As a parent of two girls, I often think about both the gifts and struggles of being a sibling. My girls share a room, pass down clothes, and go to a school where they have many of the same teachers. They will (and already do) face the challenge of always being defined over and against one another. But they also have the great gift of being friends for their whole lives; no one on earth will know them as their sister does. My prayers for them are encouraged by the example of James— may they find ways to be in relationship without resentment. May they be dedicated to one another without being defined by each other, and may they find a way to embrace their shared identity while each discovers her unique call.

Respond

To honor James of Jerusalem, celebrate others who follow Christ's pattern of vulnerable love. These "pillars" build our faith and share the love of Christ. Make a pillar to put in the center of the table. You can make your own (empty toilet paper rolls might work!) or be creative (candles, Legos, blocks, etc.).

Now, tell stories of people you've seen standing up for others or giving something up for somebody else's sake. You can prime the pump with examples of sharing or courage you've noticed with your kids, or throw in a pop culture reference— Anna in *Frozen* is a great example of self-giving love. Tell the story of James. Each person takes a turn "placing" someone on the pillar, telling their story, and giving thanks for them.

Learn More

In the Gospel according to Matthew and in the Epistle to the Galatians, the James whom we commemorate today is called the Lord's brother. Other writers, following Mark's tradition, believe him to have been a cousin of Jesus. Certain apocryphal writings speak of him as a son of Joseph's first wife. Whatever his relationship to Jesus—brother, half-brother, or cousin— James was converted after the resurrection. Eventually, he became Bishop of Jerusalem.

In the first letter to the Corinthians (15:7), Paul says that James was favored with a special appearance of the Lord before the ascension. Later, James dealt cordially with Paul at

Jerusalem, when the latter came there to meet Peter and the other apostles. During the Council of Jerusalem, when there was disagreement about whether Gentile converts should be circumcised, James summed up the momentous decision with these words: "Therefore I have reached the decision that we should not trouble those Gentiles who are turning to God" (Acts 15:19).

Eusebius, quoting from an earlier church history by Hegesippus, declares that James was surnamed "the Just." He was holy, abstemious, did not cut his hair nor oil his body, and was continually on his knees in prayer, interceding for his people. "As many as came to believe did so through James," says Hegesippus.

James's success in converting many to Christ greatly perturbed some factions in Jerusalem. According to Hegesippus, they begged him to "restrain the people, for they have gone astray to Jesus, thinking him to be the Messiah...We bear you witness that you are just...Persuade the people that they do not go astray...we put our trust in you." They then set James on the pinnacle of the temple, bidding him to preach to the multitude and turn them from Jesus. James, however, testified for the Lord. Thereupon, they hurled him from the roof to the pavement, and cudgeled him to death.

Pray

Grant, O God, that, following the example of your servant James the Just, brother of our Lord, your church may give itself continually to prayer and to the reconciliation of all who are at variance and enmity; through Jesus Christ our Lord, who lives and reigns with you and the Holy Spirit, one God, now and for ever. *Amen.*

Saint Simon and Saint Jude, Apostles

Read

Psalm 119:89-96 | Deuteronomy 32:1-4
Ephesians 2:13-22 | John 15:17-27

Reflect

I recently received a pretty cool gift. It is a button with the words: Never Too Punk Rock For Jesus.

I was a little punk rock for a season. I still have the earrings and MXPX albums to prove it. But truly, my younger brother was the epitome of punk rock. He had a mohawk that was nearly two feet tall, and his hair usually contained a rainbow of colors. He often made or altered his clothing from a patchwork of fabrics. He has always been an artsy showstopper with a certain charisma.

One time, my brother was riding in the car with my wife (they were going to pick up his tux for our wedding). They were stopped at a traffic light.

Author

Dorian Del Priore is an Episcopal priest who has been involved in youth ministry for more than twenty years. Dorian is a husband to Lauren and a father to Jordan and Brynn, and they live in Columbia, South Carolina.

The driver of another car found herself a little mesmerized by my brother's enchanting mohawk, and…BAM! She smacked right into the back of the car in front of her!

The truth is that many people often made (and still make) negative assumptions about my brother because of his appearance. But what I admire most about my brother is his deep contentment with himself. He is completely comfortable in his skin and is not worried about what other people think or feel.

I imagine each of today's saints to be much like that: comfortable and content with who they were.

We don't know too terribly much about Simon or Jude. Legends regard them as martyred in Persia. We don't know why they traveled together or what exactly drew them toward one another in their shared ministry. Simon was known as the Zealot; was Jude an opposite in personality or approach to ministry? Was Simon a hothead, more aggressive and outspoken and Jude more gentle and peaceful? There is an assumption or belief that they complemented one another in ministry.

The gospel assigned for the Feast of Saint Simon and Saint Jude comes from the fifteenth chapter of John (verses 17-27) in which Jesus tells the disciples that the world would hate them. Jesus doesn't promise accolades or favor from the world and society. Instead, he prepares the disciples to encounter tension. In essence, the disciples would be seen as misfits in tension with the established social norms and hierarchies. Sounds pretty punk rock to me.

One of the particulars that set the followers of Jesus apart from the norms of society was the command to love one another. Following Jesus and being in community with one another required communal dependence upon one another. It required a particular bond. This was, and still is, counter-cultural in many ways, and I imagine, a hallmark of the shared ministry of Simon and Jude.

We remember Simon and Jude as faithful and zealous, and I believe they remind us to have a deep appreciation and confidence in our own particular gifts. Further, they encourage an appreciation for the unique gifts, traits, and personalities of others in our community. We need not try to be something we are not, and we definitely should not try to be all things to everyone. We are simply called to be ourselves, and truly, the very best of who and what God created and intended us to be.

When we encounter Jesus, I believe we move toward becoming the very best of ourselves. Our witness to the world is that Jesus is at work in our lives: shaping, forming, and binding us together in grace, peace, and love. And that is an important reminder we receive from Simon and Jude: our need for each other binds us together as the people and kingdom of God.

Simon and Jude: maybe just enough punk rock for Jesus.

Respond

Create a prayer board, using Post-It notes, index cards, or construction paper. On each piece of paper, write the person's name along with a gift or talent that they have. Each day, pray specifically for one of the people on your prayer board, giving thanks for the gifts they offer to God and to their family and community.

Learn More

Little is known about Simon and Jude, both named in New Testament lists of the twelve disciples, but tradition has consistently associated both apostles with one another, and with missionary work in Persia and Armenia. According to most ancient authorities they were martyred together, possibly in Beirut, but accounts vary.

There are other scholarly questions about both men. One involves Simon's appellation "Zelotes" or "the Zealot." Whether in fact he had been a member before his conversion of one of the several Jewish factions called "Zealots," or whether this title refers to his zeal for the Jewish law, is not known, but he has consistently been identified by it.

Jude has long been regarded in popular devotion as the patron of desperate or lost causes. The Epistle of Jude, which is attributed to the disciple, concludes with this striking doxology: "Now to him who is able to keep you from falling, and to make you stand without blemish in the presence of his glory with rejoicing, to the only God our Savior, through Jesus Christ our Lord, be glory, majesty, power, and authority, before all time and now and forever. Amen" (Jude 24-25).

Pray

O God, we thank you for the glorious company of the apostles, and especially on this day for Simon and Jude; and we pray that, as they were faithful and zealous in their mission, so we may with ardent devotion make known the love and mercy of our Lord and Savior Jesus Christ; who lives and reigns with you and the Holy Spirit, one God, for ever and ever. *Amen.*

All Saints

Read

Psalm 34:1-10, 22 | Revelation 7:9-17
1 John 3:1-3 | Matthew 5:1-12 (Year A)

Psalm 24 | Wisdom of Solomon 3:1-9 *or* Isaiah 25:6-9
Revelation 21:1-6a | John 11:32-44 (Year B)

Psalm 149 | Daniel 7:1-3, 15-18
Ephesians 1:11-23 | Luke 6:20-31

Reflect

My boys and I adore our annual All Saints celebration. Though it varies from year to year, the celebration always includes a game we call Guess the Saint. One year we placed a few objects from around the house in a bowl to represent different saints. We had a toy bird for Francis who preached to the birds, a candle for Lucia who carried her light on her head, and

Author

Emily Watkins is headmaster of The Augustine Academy in the Milwaukee area. She loves spending days by Lake Michigan and studying nature in the Wisconsin woods with her husband and four sons.

an ox for Aquinas who was known as the dumb ox. To play the game, you pick an object out of the bowl and then get an extra clue or two as needed to see who can guess the saint the object represents. In recent years we replaced this simple bowl of objects with friends joining us for a meal where we all dress as a favorite saint and give clues to see if we can guess which saint each person has chosen to represent.

Our boys love this celebration because leftover Halloween candy is the prize when they guess a saint correctly. My children are certain they are the most sugar-deprived children in the world (they aren't), and this promise of sweets goes a long way to garner excitement.

When it comes to building our family traditions around the church year, I'm happy for enthusiasm in any form, but I also want to think about why we spend time and energy celebrating All Saints. It would be easy to focus on the fun and sugar and lose sight of why we choose to celebrate this feast day. I love the stories of the saints and feel it is important to remember them because they point us to the gospel, teach us to love, and help us to examine our own lives and grow as saints.

With every family liturgical celebration, big or small, my first goal is always to hear the gospel. The celebration of All Saints is first and foremost about the gospel. Christ has come so that we can be counted among the saints. Through the sacrifice of Christ's perfect life, we can begin the journey toward being Christ-like. To meet this goal of preaching the gospel in our celebration, we must remember who it is that makes the journey of all saints possible. It isn't something we have long discussions about, but it is our starting place.

From the lives of the saints, we learn how to love God and love others with greater fervor. These women and men who loved God and loved others well, show us the way of Jesus. I try to share lots of stories of saints during October and November. Sometimes we read through an anthology of saints at bedtime, sometimes we share a picture book over hot chocolate after school, and sometimes I hand a chapter book about a saint to my older boys and ask them to read on their own. But while what we read and when we read changes, the question I ask afterward doesn't. "I wonder how (insert saint's name here) loved God and loved others well?" Sometimes my littles' answers surprise me, reminding me that we continue to learn from the saints, even those whose stories we already know well.

When we begin to think about the gift of salvation and hear stories of people who loved God and others, a natural next step is examining our lives and pondering how we, too, can love more fully. Saints' stories prompt us to ask, "How are we loving God and others in our lives? How can we love God and others even more? Where do we fail to love God and others?" The saints will inspire us and show us the way, if we will take the time to wonder how our lives can reflect the gospel.

This year we are expanding our circle on All Saints and hosting a church-wide potluck with costumes and saintly games instead of a home celebration. I hope that other families will hear the gospel and fall in love with the stories of the saints. I pray the lives of the saints will inspire them to love God and love others with greater fervor. This is my prayer for your family, too.

Respond

Play Guess the Saint. You can start small with simple questions and clues or go all-in with a saintly dinner party and costumes. Search online for some saints quizzes or games (including catechist.com). *Meet the Saints: Family Storybook* (published by Forward Movement, best for ages 4-12) offers some great stories and downloadable coloring sheets for some of the most beloved saints, from traditional to contemporary.

Learn More

It is believed that the commemoration of all the saints on November 1 originated in Ireland, spread from there to England, and then to the European continent.

That it had reached Rome and had been adopted there early in the ninth century is attested by a letter of Pope Gregory IV, who reigned from 828 to 844, to Emperor Louis the Pious, urging that such a festival be observed throughout the Holy Roman Empire.

However, the desire of Christian people to express the intercommunion of the living and the dead in the Body of Christ by a commemoration of those who, having professed faith in the living Christ during their lives, had entered into the nearer presence of their Lord, and especially of those who had crowned their profession with heroic deaths, was far older than the early Middle Ages. Gregory Thaumaturgus (the "Wonder Worker"), writing before the year 270, refers to the observance of a festival of all martyrs, though he does not date it. A hundred years later, Ephrem the Deacon mentions such an observance in Edessa on May 13; and the patriarch John Chrysostom, who died in 407, says that a festival of All Saints was observed on the first Sunday after Pentecost in Constantinople at the time of his episcopate. The lectionary of the East Syrians set a commemoration of all the saints on Friday in Easter week. On May 13, in the year 610, the Pantheon in Rome—originally a pagan temple dedicated to "all the gods"—was dedicated as the Church of St. Mary and All Martyrs.

All Saints' Day is classified in the Prayer Book as a Principal Feast, taking precedence over any other day or observance. Among the seven Principal Feasts, All Saints' Day alone may be observed on the following Sunday, in addition to its observance on its fixed date. It is also one of the four days particularly recommended in the Prayer Book (page 312) for the administration of Holy Baptism.

Pray

Almighty God, you have knit together your elect in one communion and fellowship in the mystical body of your Son Christ our Lord: Give us grace so to follow your blessed saints in all virtuous and godly living, that we may come to those ineffable joys that you have prepared for those who truly love you; through Jesus Christ our Lord, who with you and the Holy Spirit lives and reigns, one God, in glory everlasting. *Amen.*

THANKSGIVING DAY (USA)

This date changes each year.
Check your calendar to determine the date.

Read

Psalm 65 | Deuteronomy 8:7-18 | 2 Corinthians 9:6-15
Luke 17:11-19 (Year A)

Psalm 126 | Joel 2:21-27 | 1 Timothy 2:1-7
Matthew 6:25-33 (Year B)

Psalm 100 | Deuteronomy 26:1-11
Philippians 4:4-9 | John 6:25-35 (Year C)

Author

Miriam Willard McKenney finds extreme joy in parenting her three girls: Nia, Kaia, and Jaiya. She and her husband, David, met at a Union of Black Episcopalians conference in 1981, and the family lives in Cincinnati, Ohio.

Reflect

Thanksgiving Day sat at the top of my mom's hierarchy of holidays. Her Southern cooking abilities were legendary, and on Thanksgiving, she pulled out all the stops. She'd make turkey with stuffing and giblet gravy, oyster casserole, macaroni and cheese, whipped potatoes, greens, green beans she had canned in the summer, homemade rolls, and other sundry dishes with a German chocolate pound cake and a cheesecake for dessert. The only item not homemade was the can of cranberry dressing.

Now you might be thinking, *that sounds delicious.* Or maybe you're thinking about your favorite traditional thanksgiving fixings from your childhood. Perhaps your thoughts have turned to what you're preparing or eating next week. Our holiday traditions generally revolved around food, so much so that for years after my mom's death, I refused to cook a traditional Thanksgiving dinner.

I had been scarred by years of spending hours and hours in the kitchen with mom doing whatever she asked, for however long it took: chopping carrots, onions, and celery for a roux; peeling and dicing potatoes; polishing silver; ironing tablecloths, and so on and so on. Mom wasn't in the kitchen for hours but days. And she expected me to be in there with her.

Guess what? I didn't want to be in the kitchen. I didn't want to watch her make giblet gravy. I didn't want to watch her stuff the turkey. I wanted to be anywhere doing anything except preparing for Thanksgiving.

I remember not quite getting the point of that giant meal. Why would Mom want to spend days and days planning and preparing all that food? My brothers and I didn't like half of what she fixed, and they always giggled during grace and got us all in trouble. We stuffed ourselves into a food coma that came with a huge side of dishes that had to be hand washed. I didn't give thanks for any of that at the time.

Then came the year we had to celebrate our first Thanksgiving without her. We got turkey dinners from Kroger and Whole Foods. Slowly, I began to prepare side dishes to go with the prepared turkey. Then, we began to plan and prepare non-traditional Thanksgiving dinners, where everyone, including the girls, chose at least one item for our meal. Imagine pot roast or salmon instead of turkey. We loved it, and I felt more at peace with the day.

To my surprise, in the last couple of years, I've begun to cook a more traditional meal. Growing with my girls helps me understand the joy in creating something extremely special for those you love. I do some things differently than my mom, such as give my girls more input into the menu, prepare far fewer dishes, and start cooking after my husband and I run a 10K.

But Mom's legacy lives on, especially on Thanksgiving Day. My spiritual practices of prayer and meditation help me draw on Mom's instructions on everything from preparing the roux to decorating the table. Reading the book of Exodus with my colleagues shows me that God really cares about beautiful things. So did my mom. Her Thanksgiving traditions came from love, I know that now. Every dish she prepared, she prepared with love, as her mother taught her. I'm glad I didn't miss the lesson.

Growing Christians

Respond

This Thanksgiving, let each person in the household choose a dish. It is that person's responsibility to prepare (or help make) the item. During the dinner, ask each person to explain why they chose that dish and what memories it evokes. You might consider pulling together the recipes and the memories into a family cookbook.

Learn More

Thanksgiving Day is celebrated in the United States on the fourth Thursday of November. This holiday is not only on federal calendars; *The Book of Common Prayer* lists it as a major holy day in the church calendar. The secular observance of Thanksgiving dates back to President Abraham Lincoln's proclamation to "set apart and observe the last Thursday of November next as a day of thanksgiving and praise to our beneficent Father who dwelleth in the heavens." Lincoln issued this proclamation after a woman named Sarah Josepha Hale pleaded with local, state, and national legislators to establish a national day of giving thanks. Hale had campaigned for decades before Lincoln heard her cry in the midst of the Civil War and asked the country to pause and give thanks for the blessings of peace with other countries, bountiful harvests, expansion of mines and industry, and God's mercy.

Pray

Almighty and gracious Father, we give you thanks for the fruits of the earth in their season and for the labors of those who harvest them. Make us, we pray, faithful stewards of your great bounty, for the provision of our necessities and the relief of all who are in need, to the glory of your Name; through Jesus Christ our Lord, who lives and reigns with you and the Holy Spirit, one God, now and for ever. *Amen.*

Saint Andrew the Apostle

Read

Psalm 19 *or* 19:1-6 | Deuteronomy 30:11-14
Romans 10:8b-18 | Matthew 4:18-22

Reflect

Today is the Feast of Saint Andrew the Apostle, one of Jesus' twelve apostles. We know a lot about his brother Peter, whose personality is illustrated through elaborate conversations with Jesus throughout the gospels, but little is known about Andrew. What is his character like—and who is he, other than Peter's brother?

We know from Matthew's Gospel that Andrew is a fisherman and that he and his brother Peter are fishing together in the Sea of Galilee when Jesus sees them casting their nets and speaks these famous words: "Follow me, and I will make you fish for people" (Matthew 4:19-20).

> ### Author
>
> **Erin Hougland,** an Episcopal priest in Indianapolis, loves to write, hike, camp, and spend time with her husband and two children.

It is said that the brothers "immediately" drop their nets and follow Jesus becoming the first two disciples to be called by Jesus. "Immediately," *no questions asked.* Peter later shows himself to be full of questions in his conversations with Jesus, and we who are full of questions ourselves appreciate reading Peter's dialogue, and even his disagreements, with Jesus. But Andrew, at least as it is recorded in the gospels, has little to say or ask of Jesus.

In John's Gospel, Andrew is described as a follower of John the Baptist. When Andrew hears Jesus described as "The Lamb of God" by John the Baptist, Andrew drops everything and follows Jesus. Again, *no questions asked.* In the Gospel of John, Andrew is the first disciple to be called by Jesus, the first one of the twelve to drop everything, claim Jesus as rabbi and messiah, and follow him. Also noted in John's Gospel is how Andrew is the one who brings Peter to Jesus. Andrew calls Peter to go with him and follow Jesus, claiming "We've found the Messiah" (John 1:35-42).

Both of these stories capture something about Andrew: his faith is steadfast. Andrew is clear that following Jesus is the right thing to do, *no questions asked.*

But that doesn't mean Andrew is free of doubts.

One of my favorite stories about Andrew comes from the loaves-and-fishes story in John's Gospel when the multitudes follow Jesus because they have heard of his great works and teachings. As the crowd gathers, Jesus asks his disciples how they will feed these five-thousand people. Philip is almost outraged at the question, stating that it would take more than a year to earn enough money for each person to have even one bite of food. Then Andrew chimes in, "There is a boy here who has five barley loaves and two fish. But what are they among so many people?" (John 6:9)

Andrew, bless him, sets the stage for the miracle Jesus is about to perform: the feeding of the multitudes with only five loaves of bread and two fish. Andrew seeks out a possible solution by locating some source of food that could be shared among the crowd. He doesn't scoff at the idea of feeding this massive group of people. He doesn't write it off as outrageous or impossible. Instead he follows Jesus' lead and tries to find something that would work.

But he still has his doubts.

"Here's something, Jesus," Andrew says, "but how can we make it work?" Andrew makes an effort locating resources and doing what he can to help, but he still has his doubts about how it will work.

Don't we love Andrew for his earnest attempt, the hope he holds and the doubt he shares with us in this story of feeding the multitudes?

Jesus offers his disciples what appears to be an insurmountable task, and Andrew gets on board with Jesus, holding both his faith for what Jesus promises is possible *and* his human doubts.

Today, we are faced with what feels like many insurmountable tasks: bigotry and hate filling our news cycle, humans fleeing their homelands for a better life in foreign lands, hunger and famine and disease plaguing families and children, wars and violence breaking out over political and religious ideologies. How can we hold this fear, doubt, and frustration alongside our faith in God's unconditional love and Jesus' power to heal?

Saint Andrew models this emotional work for us. Andrew holds that tension of steadfast faith and human doubt on his walk with Jesus. Andrew seeks out possible answers, seeks out gifts and resources even in the most unlikely places and brings them to Jesus. The task before the disciples appears insurmountable, but Andrew is steadfast, as if to say: "If I can find something to help and I bring it to God, I believe it will become a blessing to others."

Andrew doesn't know how the five loaves of bread and two fish belonging to a young boy will help, but he brings them to Jesus anyway. He holds tightly to his faith that Jesus will turn his offering into a blessing. Those fish will multiply into many for whoever needs nourishment, as long as he brings them forward and trusts God will provide the miracle.

We may know only a small amount about who Andrew was, but these stories paint a beautiful and full picture of what it means to follow Jesus.

We will face many impossible problems, troubles, and sorrows in this life we have been given, but that doesn't mean we give up and walk away. Saint Andrew shows us we can do something. Saint Andrew reminds us that we have gifts to offer within ourselves and others, however big or small. We can bring these gifts forward to help feed, heal and bless those around us. And like Andrew, we can hold tightly to our faith that no matter what we offer, it is enough for God to work with and make miracles happen in this broken world.

May we have the faith to bring what we have and who we are, however small it may seem, to those problems and tasks that feel so insurmountable faith and hope feel hard to come by. May we remember Saint Andrew, that even when he can't see how the problems and hardships might be addressed, he gives what he can, putting his faith in the unconditional love of Christ to do the rest with what little he has to offer. May we find it within our hearts and minds to hold fast to our faith in times of doubt and discouragement, and may we, like Saint Andrew, become beacons of light to others as we walk this journey with Jesus.

Respond

Throw your own Saint Andrew's feast!

Saint Andrew was named as Scotland's patron saint back in the fourteenth century. So today, gather your friends and feast on traditional Scottish fare: haggis, porridge, neeps (turnips), tatties (potatoes), and if you're brave enough, black pudding.

Learn More

Most biographical notes on this apostle begin "Andrew was Simon Peter's brother," and he is so described in the gospels. Identifying Andrew as Peter's brother makes it easy to know who he is, but it also makes it easy to overlook the fact of Andrew's own special gift to the company of Christ. The Gospel according to John tells how Andrew, a disciple of John the Baptist, was one of two disciples who followed Jesus after John had pointed him out, saying, "Behold the Lamb of God" (John 1:29). Andrew and the other disciple went with Jesus and stayed with him, and Andrew's first act afterward was to find his brother and bring him to Jesus. We might call Andrew the first missionary in the company of disciples.

Though Andrew was not a part of the inner circle of disciples (Peter, James, and John), he is always named in the list of disciples, and the Gospel of Matthew records Jesus' calling them from their occupation, and their immediate response to his call. Andrew was also the disciple who brought the boy with the loaves and fishes to Jesus for the feeding of the multitude.

We hear little of Andrew as a prominent leader, and he seems always to be in the shadow of Peter. Eusebius, the early church historian, records his going to Scythia, but there is no reliable information about the end of his life. Tradition has it that he was fastened to an X-shaped cross and suffered death at the hands of angry pagans. Andrew is the patron saint of Scotland.

Pray

Almighty God, who gave such grace to your apostle Andrew that he readily obeyed the call of your Son Jesus Christ, and brought his brother with him: Give unto us, who are called by your Word, grace to follow him without delay, and to bring those near to us into his gracious presence; who lives and reigns with you and the Holy Spirit, one God, now and for ever. *Amen.*

DECEMBER 21

Saint Thomas the Apostle

Read

Psalm 126 | Habakkuk 2:1-4
Hebrews 10:35-11:1 | John 20:24-29

Reflect

I was ordained on the Feast of Saint Thomas the Apostle, and it's probably just as well because, like Thomas, I often find myself vacillating between great faith and frustrating doubt.

That is why, despite desperate attempts to the contrary, I simply cannot pray the collect for Saint Thomas without a huge side-eye.

Author

Marcus Halley is an Episcopal priest serving as dean of formation for the Diocese of Connecticut.

Saint Thomas's most famous New Testament episode takes place a few days after the resurrection when he misses Jesus' first appearance among the disciples who were holed up in the Upper Room. We aren't told where Thomas was, only that he wasn't with the others. When the other ten disciples tell Thomas what has happened, Thomas famously says, "Unless I see the mark of the nails in his hands, and put my finger in the mark of the nails and my hand in his side, I will not believe." A week later, the disciples, not satisfied with having seen the resurrected Lord once, are still locked in the Upper Room when the Lord walks through the wall. This time, Thomas is with them. Jesus' response is one of great importance. He invites Thomas to touch him.

When I think of this event, I picture what Caravaggio captured in his painting, "The Incredulity of Saint Thomas." Thomas leans in closely, examining the Risen Lord as if he were a science project. Jesus, fully aware of our human frailty, pulls aside his clothes as if to assist Thomas in his inspection. Having satisfied his curiosity, Thomas declares, "My Lord and my God!" Jesus responds by saying, "Thomas you believe because you have seen me. Blessed are those who have not seen and yet believe."

Too often, we read this statement as an indictment against Thomas. Maybe it was. But what if it wasn't? What if Jesus was affirming Thomas? What if Jesus was willing to do what must be done to help Thomas lean into his doubt in order to midwife a deeper sense of faith? What if Jesus enters our own spaces of doubt to invite each of us into a deeper relationship?

I have worked with children long enough to know that children ask a lot of questions. Unfortunately, the wonder that seems natural for children is squeezed out of us as we age by a world in search of quick and easy answers. Against this temptation, I hear Jesus' famous words, "Truly I tell you, unless you change and become like children, you will never enter the kingdom of heaven." Jesus invites us into wonder and questioning.

Holy scripture is nothing if it is not filled with wonder. Giant fish. Walls of water. Burning bushes. Talking donkeys. Choirs of angels. Great dragons. What would happen if we read scripture as a family and suspended disbelief long enough to enter the new world presented in the text? What if we engaged the written Word of God, not as something meant to be swallowed whole but as a sumptuous morsel of the kingdom of heaven meant to be savored and enjoyed? Pick a story like the Exodus or David and Goliath. Read it. Enter the words. Explore them. Pick them up. Inspect them. Play with them. Draw. Act. Sing. Have fun.

Thomas stuck his finger into the wounds of Christ and so believed. Perhaps we are called to enter the Words of Christ and do the same, not by ignoring doubt but by hearing God's call to go where we have never gone before.

Respond

As a way to honor Thomas and his questions and curiosity, create a Dinnertime Question Jar. All you need is a minimally decorated mason jar (or other container) and some slips of paper in three colors (blue: everyone; purple: kids ask adults; orange: adults ask kids). Each slip holds a single question, one that is designed for more than a simple yes-or-no response. The question jar can help lead to a story that will further each of our understandings of one another and deepen our relationships. For a list of suggested questions, visit GrowChristians.org/holydays.

Growing Christians

Learn More

The Gospel according to John records several incidents in which Thomas appears, and from them we are able to gain some impression of the sort of man he was. When Jesus insisted on going to Judea, to visit his friends at Bethany, Thomas boldly declared, "Let us also go, that we may die with him" (John 11:16). At the Last Supper, he interrupted our Lord's discourse with the question, "Lord, we do not know where you are going; how can we know the way?" (John 14:5). And after Christ's resurrection, Thomas would not accept the account of the women and the other apostles, until Jesus himself appeared before him, showing him his wounds. This drew from him the first explicit acknowledgment of Christ's divinity, "My Lord and my God!" (John 20:28).

Thomas appears to have been a thoughtful if perhaps literal-minded man, inclined to skepticism; but he was a staunch friend when his loyalty was once given. The expression "Doubting Thomas," which has become established in English usage, is not entirely fair to Thomas. He did not refuse belief: he wanted to believe, but did not dare, without further evidence. Because of his goodwill, Jesus gave him a sign, although Jesus had refused a sign to the Pharisees. His Lord's rebuke was well deserved: "Blessed are those who have not seen and yet have come to believe" (John 20:29). The sign did not create faith; it merely released the faith that was in Thomas already.

According to an early tradition mentioned by Eusebius and others, Thomas evangelized the Persians. Syrian Christians of

India cherish a tradition that after his mission to Persia, he continued East and brought the gospel to India. The site of his burial, in present-day Chennai, has been a shrine and place of Christian pilgrimage since antiquity.

Thomas's honest questioning and doubt, and Jesus' assuring response to him, have given many modern Christians courage to persist in faith, even when they are still doubting and questioning.

Pray

Everliving God, who strengthened your apostle Thomas with firm and certain faith in your Son's resurrection: Grant us so perfectly and without doubt to believe in Jesus Christ, our Lord and our God, that our faith may never be found wanting in your sight; through him who lives and reigns with you and the Holy Spirit, one God, now and for ever. *Amen.*

The Nativity of Our Lord Jesus Christ

Read

Psalm 96 | Isaiah 9:2-7 | Titus 2:11-14
Luke 2:1-14,(15-20) (Year A)

Psalm 97 | Isaiah 62:6-12 | Titus 3:4-7
Luke 2:(1-7), 8-20 (Year B)

Psalm 98 | Isaiah 52:7-10 | Hebrews 1:1-4,(5-12)
John 1:1-14 (Year C)

Reflect

John 3:16 may be my favorite verse: "For God so loved the world that he gave his only Son, so that everyone who believes in him may not perish but may have eternal life." It binds together faith and hope and love. But do I really believe it? Is it possible that God exists? Is it possible that God wants to connect with me and that through acceptance I can connect to the love that is God?

Certainly many people do not believe there is a God. Of those who believe a God exists, not everyone believes that

> **Author**
>
> **Mary Ann Frishman** and her husband have two grown children and reside in Austin, Texas.

Jesus was God made man and lived on this earth and that we can be in communion with God through the Holy Spirit in us. Why should I believe?

I've read arguments for and against God. Bumper stickers mock faith as fiction, encouraging us to trust in ourselves and our quest of knowledge through science. Despite all this, I believe. I believe in God the Father, Jesus, his only son, and in the Holy Spirit. I would like to say I believe wholeheartedly all the time, but my faith is just a glimmer of what I hope it will be one day.

What I can say today is that I sense God's majesty in the unquestionable beauty of the natural world around me. I feel love in the tenderness of a parent's gaze into the eyes of their child. I connect to God's power in the will of someone's effort to make things better. I rest in the comfort of God's love though my closest connections. And my husband and I share our experience of faith with our children.

My version of the "12 Days of Christmas" is my statement of faith: it starts with the acceptance that God is real and wants a relationship with me and extends to how that belief needs to take shape in my life, day to day. I need to seek and study and pray. I need to be grateful and share and follow. I need to love and connect.

Respond

Using leftover boxes, wrapping paper, and ribbon, make a memory box for your family. Place an item or two—maybe a picture of something special that happened this year or an item you collected—in the box with a short note explaining its meaning or importance. Put the box away with the Christmas decorations to be opened next year.

Another way to respond to today's celebration is to write thank-you notes, including one to Jesus.

Learn More

That Jesus was born is a fact both of history and revelation. The precise date of his birth, however, is not recorded in the gospels, which are, after all, not biographies, and show little concern for those biographical details in which more modern Christians are interested. Such interest began to become prominent in the fourth century, together with the development of liturgical observances concerning the events of biblical history.

Scholars have offered various theories about how December 25 came to be selected as the date for the liturgical commemoration of the Nativity in the Western Church. An older scholarly view suggests that the date, coming as it does at the winter solstice, was already a sacred one, being observed by Roman pagans as the festival of the birth of the Unconquerable Sun (*dies natalis Solis Invicti*). This correspondence is noted by some early Christian writers themselves, who see it as a fitting parallel, but the pagan celebration was only established in the late third century, and the Christian observance of December 25 seems to have even earlier antecedents.

An alternative explanation calculates the date of Christmas based on the date of Passover and Easter. Many early Christian theologians, particularly in North Africa, calculated that the crucifixion had taken place on the 14 of Nisan, which worked out to be March 25 on the Roman calendar. This date also became celebrated as the Feast of the Annunciation because of a widespread pious belief that Jesus died on the same date that he was conceived, showing how deeply interconnected all of the events of salvation history were. December 25, then, becomes the date of Christ's birth, because it is exactly nine months after the date of his conception. This method of calculating also explains the traditional dating in the Eastern church, which historically fixed the Nativity on January 6 rather than December 25. The Eastern church calculated the date of both annunciation and crucifixion using not the 14 of Nisan, but rather the 14 of Artemisios, the first spring month on the Greek calendar. This translates to April 6 on the Roman calendar, which is nine months before January 6.

The full title of the feast dates from the 1662 edition of *The Book of Common Prayer*. Prior to that revision, the day was known only as "Christmas Day." The word "Christmas," which can be traced to the twelfth century, is a contraction of "Christ's Mass."

Growing Christians

Pray

Almighty God, you have given your only-begotten Son to take our nature upon him, and to be born [this day] of a pure virgin: Grant that we, who have been born again and made your children by adoption and grace, may daily be renewed by your Holy Spirit; through our Lord Jesus Christ, to whom with you and the same Spirit be honor and glory, now and for ever. *Amen.*

Saint Stephen, Deacon and Martyr

Read

Psalm 31 *or* 31:1-5 | Jeremiah 26:1-9,12-15
Acts 6:8—7:1-7:2a, 51c-60 | Matthew 23:34-39

Reflect

Today we celebrate the life of Saint Stephen, whose dramatic story unfolds in the book of Acts. If you aren't familiar with Stephen's life, let me set the stage for you.

Author
Allison Sandlin Liles is a wife, mother, peacemaker, and priest learning how to navigate life in the suburban wilds of Dallas, Texas.

Stephen has been chosen as one of seven men to lead the early Christians living in Jerusalem. We learn in the sixth and seventh chapters of Acts that Stephen is a good man and full of faith, love, and the Holy Spirit. He oversees the money used to care for widows, orphans, and other people living on the fringes of society.

All is well until he challenges a group of Jews from Cyrene, Alexandria, Cilicia, and Asia gathered at the synagogue. They engage in a theological debate, and Stephen wins. Acts 6:10 says these Jewish leaders "could not withstand the wisdom and the Spirit with which he spoke." Humiliated and angry, they decide to defame Stephen's character by hiring false witnesses to say that they had heard Stephen speak blasphemous words against Moses and God. This stirs up the people, the elders, and the scribes who capture Stephen and bring him to a trial in a Jewish court.

During the trial, Stephen delivers a long speech in his defense. He recites a history of Jewish people being disobedient to God, including Abraham, Isaac, Jacob, and Joseph, Moses, David… it goes on and on and on and until suddenly, in verse fifty-one of chapter seven, there's a change. The historical reflections on Hebrew heroes are abruptly replaced with this personal attack:

> You stiff-necked people, uncircumcised in heart and ears, you are forever opposing the Holy Spirit, just as your ancestors used to do. Which of the prophets did your ancestors not persecute? They killed those who foretold the coming of the Righteous One, and now you have become his betrayers and murderers. You are the ones that received the law as ordained by angels, and yet you have not kept it (Acts 7:51-53).

Stephen speaks harshly to those gathered at his trial; it does not go over well. They drag Stephen outside of the city and mercilessly start stoning him. While dying, Stephen prays for his killers: "Lord, do not hold this sin against them." Soon, Stephen's body is silent and lifeless. He becomes the first martyr of our church.

Stephen's honesty leaves me stunned. I learned early in my Alabama childhood to sugarcoat the truth to get what I wanted from others—almost manipulating my intended target. The phrase, "You catch more flies with honey than vinegar" was a refrain repeated frequently in my household. This thought never even occurs to Stephen. He doesn't hide behind manipulation, nor does he tiptoe around the issues bothering him. Stephen instead chooses to speak the unmasked truth despite the obvious threat of consequences.

Young children's interpersonal skills are often as brazenly honest as Stephen's. As a three-year-old, my daughter Pailet ensured my humility with her outspoken opinions about my hair, my renditions of Taylor Swift songs, my choice of clothes, and the dark circles under my eyes that magically appeared some mornings.

Then a year ago, she stopped. Somewhere around ages four or five, we teach our children that they should not say every single thought that pops into their heads. We teach them to think of other people's feelings and what it means to be empathetic.

As we celebrate Stephen's life today, I wonder about the disservice we are doing our children with these life lessons. I cannot say that I miss my daughter's running commentary on my looks and parenting skills, but I do miss hearing what's on her mind. I want my children to be kind and considerate, but I also want them to speak the truth courageously.

There is a lot of middle ground between manipulating people to get what you want and being so direct that you end up a martyr. We are living in that middle ground right now, but every day we nudge our children back toward their bold toddler truth-telling.

Respond

In remembrance of Stephen's work for the needy, the British people have a tradition to collect money throughout the year in little clay boxes. On the feast of Saint Stephen or "Boxing Day" as it is called in Britain, these boxes are broken, and the money distributed to the poor. (This is the origin of the "piggy bank.") In some homes and communities, a box is labeled and set beside the Christmas tree. Members of the family, in gratitude for their Christmas blessings, choose one of their gifts for the "Saint Stephen's Box"—clothing and other useful articles are sent abroad to the poor or to a mission country. Consider creating your own Saint Stephen's box and donate to a local social service organization.

Learn More

Very probably a Hellenistic Jew, Stephen was one of the "seven men of good repute, full of the Spirit and of wisdom" (Acts 6:3), who were chosen by the apostles to relieve them of the administrative burden of "serving tables and caring for the widows." By this appointment to assist the apostles, Stephen, the first named of those the New Testament calls "The Seven," became the first to do what the church traditionally considers to be the work and ministry of a deacon.

It is apparent that Stephen's activities involved more than simply "serving tables," however, for the Acts of the Apostles speaks of his preaching and performing many miracles. These activities led him into conflict with some of the Jews, who accused him of blasphemy, and brought him before the Sanhedrin. His powerful sermon before the Council is recorded in the seventh chapter of Acts. According to this account, his denunciations of the Sanhedrin so enraged its members that, without a trial, they dragged him out of the city and stoned him to death. Stephen is traditionally regarded as the very first Christian martyr.

Saul, later called Paul, stood by, consenting to Stephen's death, but Stephen's example of steadfast faith in Jesus, and of intercession for his persecutors, was to find fruit in the mission and witness of Paul after his conversion. The Christian community in Jerusalem, taking fright at the hostility of the Judean authorities, was scattered, so that for the first time the gospel of Christ began to spread beyond Jerusalem.

Pray

We give you thanks, O Lord of glory, for the example of the first martyr Stephen, who looked up to heaven and prayed for his persecutors to your Son Jesus Christ, who stands at your right hand; where he lives and reigns with you and the Holy Spirit, one God, in glory everlasting. *Amen.*

Growing Christians

Saint John, Apostle and Evangelist

Read

Psalm 92 *or* 92:1-4,11-14 | Exodus 33:18-23
1 John 1:1-9 | John 21:19b-24

Reflect

On this third day of Christmas, we may be feeling a bit let down. The reflection and waiting of Advent is over. We may or may not have found time and space for that much-needed slowing down in the midst of concerts and parties and presents and stockings hung by the chimney with care. The kids are home from school, wrapping paper and bits of ribbon still litter the floors, and new toys, long begged-for and dreamt-of, are on the way to losing their luster. When my boys were little, by today at least one new toy was already broken. Too much food sits in our bellies and our refrigerators, and the rest of the school break looms.

Author

Christina (Tina) Clark lives in Denver, Colorado, has two teenage sons, and loves all things church, the Rocky Mountains, and the Pacific Ocean.

But today is the feast of Saint John the Evangelist, and if anyone can show us the way to Christ, it is the disciple whom Jesus loved.

The next day, John [the Baptist] was again standing with two of his disciples, and as he watched Jesus walk by, he exclaimed, "Look, here is the Lamb of God!" The two disciples heard him say this, and they followed Jesus. When Jesus turned and saw them following, he said to them, "What are you looking for?" (John 1:35-38)

The answer given by the disciple John in the rest of that last verse is, "Rabbi... where are you staying?"

That's the socially correct answer to Jesus' question. But sometimes I think I know what was in John's heart in that moment, what he longed to cry out in answer: "You, dear Jesus, we're looking for you! We're looking for love and joy and salvation and righteousness. We're looking for the Messiah that was foretold, and we know that it's you."

They spend the rest of the afternoon with Jesus, and that's it for John. He's hooked. He believes; he knows that he has found the Christ, and nothing but Jesus' directions will take him away from that blessed companionship.

As the detritus of Christmas surrounds us, where do we see Jesus? How do we help our children translate the beauty of the baby born to Mary to the man John clung to in such love and devotion? How do we help them conflate the joys of Christmas with their relationship with God through Christ?

Maybe the next time our children start bickering—and if that doesn't happen during the long school vacations at your house, I'm happy to send my boys over for a day or two—we can tell

Growing Christians

them about John's mother. She knelt before Jesus and dared to ask him to promise that her two sons would sit at his right and left hands in the kingdom of heaven (Matthew 20:20-28). I wonder if we think she was brave to ask that.

I wonder how John felt when his mother asked Jesus for that promise. (My ten-year-old would probably collapse in a paroxysm of embarrassment.)

I wonder how the other disciples felt when they heard about it. The Bible tells us they were angry, but Jesus said something we can spend time talking and thinking about: "Whoever wishes to be great among you must be your servant, and whoever wishes to be first among you must be your slave; just as the Son of Man came not to be served but to serve, and to give his life a ransom for many" (Matthew 20:26-28).

I wonder what Jesus means about being each other's servant or slave. What twenty-first-century words can we use to describe how Christ wants us to treat each other?

I wonder how we can find ways to serve one another, remembering that in this Christmas season, we are celebrating the birth of Christ, who came to teach us to love God and to love each other.

Maybe the story and the time coming up with ideas will calm the Christmas chaos, at least for a few minutes.

Glory to God in the highest, and on earth peace and goodwill to all people.

Respond

At dinner tonight, light a candle for Christ and then say, "I wonder what we would do or say if Jesus came to eat turkey leftovers with us." Children will wonder about Jesus at various ages; encourage that conversation. What if Jesus came to visit and he was the same age as the children at the table? How would they welcome him? How would it be the same and different than having their school friends over for dinner?

Learn More

John, the son of Zebedee, with his brother James, was called from being a fisherman to be a disciple and "fisher of men." With Peter and James, he became one of the inner group of three disciples whom Jesus chose to be with him at the raising of Jairus' daughter, at the Transfiguration, and in the garden of Gethsemane.

John and his brother James are recorded in the gospel as being so hotheaded and impetuous that Jesus nicknamed them *Boanerges*, which means sons of thunder. They also appear ambitious, in that they sought seats of honor at Jesus' right and left when he should come into his kingdom. Yet they were also faithful companions, willing, without knowing the cost, to share the cup Jesus was to drink. When the other disciples responded in anger to the audacity of the brothers in asking for this honor, Jesus explained that in his kingdom leadership and rule take the form of being a servant to all.

If, as is commonly held, John is to be identified with the "disciple whom Jesus loved," then he clearly enjoyed a very special relationship with his Master, reclining close to Jesus at the Last Supper, receiving the care of his mother at the cross, and being the first to understand the truth of the empty tomb.

The Acts of the Apostles records John's presence with Peter on several occasions: the healing of the lame man at the Beautiful Gate of the Temple, before the Sanhedrin, in prison, and on the mission to Samaria to lay hands upon the new converts that they might receive the Holy Spirit.

According to tradition, John later went to Asia Minor and settled at Ephesus. Under the Emperor Domitian, he was exiled to the island of Patmos, where he experienced the visions recounted in the Book of Revelation. Irenaeus, at the end of the second century, liked to recall how Polycarp, in his old age, had talked about the apostle whom he had known while growing up at Ephesus. It is probable that John died there. He alone of the Twelve is said to have lived to extreme old age and to have been spared a martyr's death.

Pray

Shed upon your church, O Lord, the brightness of your light, that we, being illumined by the teaching of your apostle and evangelist John, may so walk in the light of your truth, that at length we may attain to the fullness of eternal life; through Jesus Christ our Lord, who lives and reigns with you and the Holy Spirit, one God, for ever and ever. *Amen.*

December 28

Holy Innocents

Read

Psalm 124 | Jeremiah 31:15-17
Revelation 21:1-7 |Matthew 2:13-18

Reflect

The biblical story of the Holy Innocents is told in Matthew 2:13-18 with Herod's death squad murdering all children age two and younger living in and around Bethlehem because the wise men told him a king was born there while they were following the star.

Author
Allison Sandlin Liles is a wife, mother, peacemaker, and priest learning how to navigate life in the suburban wilds of Dallas, Texas.

It's an unsettling story, to say the least.

Was Herod mentally ill? Did he want to hold onto his power, position, or wealth? There are always so many unanswered "why did he do it" questions after mass murders. All we know from Matthew's text is that Herod decided children must die, and thus children were killed.

The Feast of the Holy Innocents is not a day that lends itself to traditional family celebrations. Today I am not offering you craft projects to create with grandparents who are still in town or recipes to prepare in the warmth of kitchens you have used so much over the past few days. Instead, today I ask you to consider all the innocent children who continue dying at the hands of greed, power, hatred, and injustice and to ask what you are doing to ensure fewer parents know such pain.

Who are our contemporary Holy Innocents?

It's estimated that Herod ordered the deaths of 14,000 babies and toddlers the week after Jesus' birth. This number seems unfathomable. Or at least it does until we put it into a modern context. Since the massacre at Sandy Hook Elementary in Newtown, Connecticut, on December 14, 2012, nearly this many children and teenagers have died by gunshot. According to the Brady Campaign to Prevent Gun Violence, every day, forty-eight children and teens are shot in murders, assaults, suicides and suicide attempts, unintentional shootings, and police intervention.

Every day, seven children and teens die from gun violence. These are our Holy Innocents.

Abroad we look no further than Aleppo, Syria, to see numbers of innocent children dying at rates comparable to Herod's time. The images we've seen are heartbreaking. Parents carrying the limp bodies of their babies. Children wailing over their siblings' body bags. A stunned five-year-old boy covered in dust and blood sitting with his feet dangling over the edge of an ambulance seat. Rather than being raised to a soundtrack of education, laughter, and outdoor exploration, the children of Aleppo are saddled with the sounds of constant gunfire, explosions, and weeping. These are our Holy Innocents.

So as parents, what do we do?

I encourage you to use the extra time you have with your children over winter break to explore the lives of modern-day Holy Innocents. It could be the children dying in Aleppo or the American children dying from our country's addiction to firearms. It could be the world's 10 million children under five who die annually from malnutrition or hunger-related causes or the 1.2 million children who are trafficked each year around the world. Learn some of their stories. Learn some of the contributing factors to their deaths. Learn what you can do to ensure fewer parents know such pain.

I will spend today with my five- and seven-year-olds exploring the lives of children sacrificed on the altar our country has created out of guns. We will write letters to our newly elected congressperson asking him to support gun law reforms like universal background checks, extreme risk protection orders, and restricting access to high capacity magazines.

We will once again revisit our family's rules on playing with toy guns and always asking about unlocked guns before visiting someone else's home. And we will pray, pray, pray.

We must remember that the problems facing Jesus and the Hebrew prophets involved public issues such as economic justice, relief for widows, orphans, and refugees, and fair treatment of all those living on the fringes of society.... addressing the suffering of the innocents.

The suffering of innocent human beings is a religious issue. Relieving such suffering is an imperative of our faith.

Respond

Visit the Episcopal Relief & Development website with your household and learn what they are doing for children around the world. Is there a particular effort that your children are passionate about supporting? Find your local Episcopal Relief & Development Ministry Partner and inquire how you can actively support their programs. Visit episcopalrelief.org/children to learn more.

Learn More

Herod the Great, ruler of the Jews, appointed by the Romans in 40 BCE, kept the peace in Palestine for thirty-seven years. His ruthless control, coupled with genuine ability, has been recorded by the Jewish historian Josephus, who describes him as "a man of great barbarity toward everyone." An Idumaean, married to the daughter of Hyrcanus, the last legal Hasmonean ruler, Herod was continually in fear of losing his throne. It is not surprising that the Magi's report of the birth of an infant King of the Jews (Matthew 2) would have caused him fear and anger. Although the event is not recorded in secular history, the story of the massacre of the Innocents would have been in keeping with what is known of Herod's character.

To protect himself against being supplanted by an infant king, Herod ordered the slaughter of all male children under two years of age in Bethlehem and the surrounding region. From antiquity, the church has consistently honored these innocent children as martyrs, even though they were quite obviously not Christians, because they were killed by one who was seeking to destroy Christ.

Augustine of Hippo called them "buds, killed by the frost of persecution the moment they showed themselves."

Pray

We remember today, O God, the slaughter of the holy innocents of Bethlehem by King Herod. Receive, we pray, into the arms of your mercy all innocent victims; and by your great might frustrate the designs of evil tyrants and establish your rule of justice, love, and peace; through Jesus Christ our Lord, who lives and reigns with you, in the unity of the Holy Spirit, one God, for ever and ever. *Amen.*

About the Contributors

Meaghan Brower serves as the executive director of the Episcopal Conference Center (ECC), the summer camp and retreat center for the Diocese of Rhode Island. After graduating from Virginia Theological Seminary in 2007, Meaghan worked as the associate rector at Emmanuel Church in Southern Pines, North Carolina. From there, she and her husband Jonathan took some time off to travel and discern God's will in their lives. They were delighted that their discernment brought them back to their home state of Rhode Island and to the camp where they met. Meaghan has worked at ECC since 2012. She lives in Newport with Jonathan, a furniture maker, and their three children.

Christina (Tina) Clark serves as director of Christian Formation at Saint John's Cathedral in Denver, Colorado, and is the author of the resource book *Arts Camp: A Creative, Customizable Alternative to Vacation Bible School and Beyond* and of the novel *Little Gods on Earth*. Tina lives in Denver, has two teenage sons, and loves all things church, the Rocky Mountains, and the Pacific Ocean. Tina's calling is to create meaningful formational experiences for all ages, from Godly Play for little ones about to be baptized to exploring all aspects of faith with teens and adults. A staunch advocate for social justice, Tina yearns to walk every day in the Baptismal Covenant to seek and serve Christ by striving for justice and peace among all people and respecting the dignity of every human being...even the ones with whom she ardently disagrees.

Ben Day is the rector of Christ Episcopal Church in Kennesaw, Georgia. He is an avid reader, cyclist, and runner. He is also a single father to a young son, Marshall. They share their home with two rescue dogs, Becket and Augustine—both named after Archbishops of Canterbury!

Dorian Del Priore is an Episcopal priest currently serving as the canon for mission and evangelism at Trinity Cathedral in Columbia, South Carolina. A graduate of the University of South Carolina and Virginia Theological Seminary, he has been involved in youth ministry for more than twenty years. Dorian is a husband to Lauren and a father to Jordan and Brynn. They have a particular heart for rescuing Great Danes. He loves photography, swimming, hiking, camping, and ice cream, especially butter pecan.

Ann Benton Fraser is a priest serving as an associate rector at historic St. Mark's in downtown San Antonio, Texas. She lives with her husband Andrew, who is a fellow Louisiana native, and their three children (two Mississippians and a Texan). She spends time reading, being outside, and learning from her children. Either indecisive or decidedly adaptable, she likes *Game of Thrones* and *Call the Midwife,* using scissors and glue, making messes and cleaning up messes, quiet and chaos, and things Protestant and Catholic.

Mary Ann Frishman is the owner and president of Frishco, Ltd, an editorial development house that focuses on the development of pre-k through twelfth grade textbooks and ancillary educational materials. Mary Ann holds undergraduate and graduate degrees from the University of

Texas at Austin. She is deeply connected to her community, helping to establish Hillside Early Childhood Center and volunteering with the Gazelle Foundation, the Helping Hand Home Society, and the Seton Development Board. She and her husband have two grown children and reside in Austin, Texas.

Patrick Funston is husband to Michael and father to Eirnín and York. Patrick serves the Diocese of Kansas as canon to the ordinary. He has also served parish and chaplaincy roles. Patrick, an avid gamer and geek, especially loves the preaching and teaching aspects of his ministry.

Marcus Halley is an Episcopal priest serving as dean of formation for the Diocese of Connecticut. He holds a bachelor of arts degree from Johnson C. Smith University, a master of divinity degree from the Interdenominational Theological Center, and a master of sacred theology from the School of Theology at the University of the South. An avid writer and blogger, Marcus has contributed to numerous other publications both online and in print.

Erin Hougland is the Pathways to Vitality priest for the Episcopal Diocese of Indianapolis. As the Pathways priest, Erin works with three congregations over a two-year period to help develop their discipleship pathways and programming, stewardship and regular giving campaigns, ministry organization and structure as well as evangelism and outreach initiatives. Erin comes from Kentucky originally but has lived in Indianapolis since 2008. She loves to write, hike, camp, and spend time with her husband and two children. Erin received her bachelor's degree in theological studies from Hanover

College in 2008, her master of divinity from Earlham School of Religion in 2014, and her diploma for Anglican studies from Bexley Seabury Seminary Federation in Chicago in 2017. Erin is passionate about fostering a sense of spiritual knowing within individuals and faith communities and believes our capacity to share love and compassion will save, heal, and transform us into the beacons of hope and light God has made us to be.

Sara Irwin was ordained in the Episcopal Church in 2004 and serves as pastor of St. John Evangelical Lutheran Church in Carnegie, five miles south of Pittsburgh, Pennsylvania. She is mother to Isaiah and Adah, and spouse to Noah Evans, rector of St. Paul's Episcopal Church, Mt. Lebanon. She loves tattoos, hiking, and making beer. She writes for *Mt. Lebanon Magazine* and other publications. Her blog is at saraiwrites. blogspot.com.

Lauren Kuratko is an Episcopal priest and mother in the Diocese of New York. As a spiritual director, she enjoys looking for God in the humor (and humdrum!) of everyday life and community. Lauren is the rector of Grace Episcopal Church in Hastings-on-Hudson, New York. Lauren enjoys outdoor adventures with her husband and three exuberant boys, every single second of quiet she can find, and cheering for Auburn football.

Allison Sandlin Liles is a wife, mother, peacemaker, and priest learning how to navigate life in the suburban wilds of Dallas, Texas. After working as executive director of the Episcopal Peace Fellowship for six years, Allison has re-entered parish ministry in the Diocese of Fort Worth. She currently serves as the priest in charge of St. Stephen's Episcopal Church in Hurst, Texas.

Miriam Willard McKenney finds extreme joy in parenting her three girls: Nia, Kaia, and Jaiya. She and her husband, David, met at the Union of Black Episcopalians conference in 1981, and the family lives in Cincinnati, Ohio. Miriam works as Forward Movement's Development Director and is on the Way of Love working group. She was a children's librarian and school media specialist for twenty years before joining Forward Movement's staff. She loves to evangelize about her love of outdoor fitness, even in extreme temperatures—as there is no bad weather, just incorrect clothing choices.

Derek Olsen is a layman within the Episcopal Church with a doctorate in New Testament. He is the liturgical editor of the *Saint Augustine's Prayer Book* and the author of *Inwardly Digest: The Prayer Book as Guide to a Spiritual Life*. Derek has served on the Episcopal Church's Standing Commission for Liturgy & Music. An IT professional by day, he is also the mastermind behind St Bede Productions, which is responsible for the St Bede's Breviary, Forward Movement's Daily Prayer site, and the St Bede Blog (formerly haligweorc). He lives in Baltimore, Maryland, with his wife, an Episcopal priest, and their two daughters.

Nurya Love Parish is an Episcopal priest and ministry developer and was the founding editor of *Grow Christians*. She currently serves as founding executive director of Plainsong Farm, a new mission agency of the Episcopal Church, and rector of Holy Spirit Episcopal Church, both in Michigan. She has reached the late teenage stage of parenting with her firefighter husband.

Genevieve Razim is grateful for the generations of church folk who have shared the faith with her. As an Episcopal priest in the Diocese of Texas, she prays for the grace to do the same. Married for twenty-five years and the mother of two young men, her favorite place to be is at the table with loved ones.

Melody Wilson Shobe is an Episcopal priest who serves as associate for children and families at Church of the Good Shepherd in Dallas, Texas. A graduate of Tufts University and Virginia Theological Seminary, Melody has authored and co-authored a number of books and curricula for Forward Movement, including *Faithful Questions, Meet the Saints: A Family Storybook, The Path: A Family Storybook,* and *Walk in Love: Episcopal Beliefs & Practices.* Melody, her husband, and their two daughters live in Dallas, Texas, where she spends her spare time reading stories, building forts, conquering playgrounds, and exploring nature.

Heather Sleightholm is an artist, wife, and mother living in northeastern Oklahoma. She sells her paintings through her folk art business and recently illustrated the book *Mary Holds My Hand* by Michele Chronister. You can read more about her art and exploration of faith through her paintbrush at sleightholmfolk.com

Emily Watkins has a master's degree in applied theology from Regent College in Vancouver and is the headmaster of The Augustine Academy, a hybrid Charlotte Mason School in the Milwaukee area. She loves spending days by Lake Michigan and studying nature in the Wisconsin woods with her husband and four sons.

Carrie Willard lives in Houston, Texas, with her husband, two sons, three dogs, and a cat who showed up on her front step one day. Carrie is an attorney who works in university administration. Her writing also appears in *Mockingbird* and *The Anglican Digest.* Carrie and her family attend Palmer Memorial Episcopal Church in Houston.

About Forward Movement

Forward Movement inspires disciples and empowers evangelists. While we produce great resources like this book, Forward Movement is not a publishing company.

We are a discipleship ministry. Publishing books, daily reflections, studies for small groups, and online resources are important ways we live out this ministry. People around the world read daily devotions through *Forward Day by Day*, which is also available in Spanish (*Adelante Dia a Dia*) and Braille, online, as a podcast, and as an app for your smartphone. We actively seek partners across the church and look for ways to provide resources that inspire and challenge. A ministry of the Episcopal Church since 1935, Forward Movement is a nonprofit organization funded by sales of resources and gifts from generous donors.

To learn more about Forward Movement and our work, visit us at forwardmovement.org or venadelante.org. We are delighted to be doing this work and invite your prayers and support.